Michael Paul Gallagher SJ

Questions
of Faith

VERITAS

First published 1996 by
Veritas Publications
7-8 Lower Abbey Street
Dublin 1

ISBN 1 85390 234 9

British Library Cataloguing
in Publication Data.
A catalogue record for
this book is available
from the British Library.

Cover design by Banahan McManus Ltd, Dublin
Internal typography by Bill Bolger
Printed in the Republic of Ireland by Betaprint, Dublin

CONTENTS

PART III

Understanding Faith

Getting Rid of Buckets

These pages are born both from people and from books, but in that order. The outer story of my own life has been fairly academic: after more than ten years of university study, I ended up lecturing in English in University College, Dublin for nearly twenty years. Then I went to Rome, where I worked in the Vatican for five years, mainly in a research capacity, in the Pontifical Council for Dialogue with Non-Believers, which became the Pontifical Council for Culture in 1993. Now I teach theology for half the year in the Gregorian University in Rome.

All that means is that I've spent a lot of my life with books. But I've also spent thousands of hours with people, especially with young people, listening to them searching to make sense of themselves or of God. Even in my Vatican years I continued to do that through the chaplaincy of Europe's biggest university, La Sapienza in Rome, with a mere 160,000 students!

I would like this book to reach young adults who have questions about Christian faith, and I hope it will also be of interest to people of other generations who want to revisit some of the basics of faith. They could do this of course through many bigger and more ambitious books, including *The Catechism of the Catholic Church*. This shorter treatment deliberately aims at a more pastoral and personal wavelength of communication. It tries to provoke the reader into thinking and, indeed, praying through these large questions. No doubt there are many people today for whom the whole 'faith thing' seems simply unreal and irrelevant. If this book comes into their hands, I would say to them: give yourselves a chance to *get inside* these questions – otherwise my answers will seem like a foreign language.

These sections tackle some twenty-five major issues, offering brief answers that are, hopefully, not too skimpy or superficial. These pages should not be hard to read, and yet they should not be too easy either. The topics chosen are not the controversial ones that create newspaper headlines – priestly celibacy, women priests, Vatican policy on bishops, Church control in education or in society, abortion, contraception, divorce, religious tensions and scandals, and so on. This is partly because my own interests in theology lie elsewhere, but more so because I think crucial questions of faith can get smothered by the more burning issues of the day.

So these questions and answers deal with a selected number of basic issues for understanding faith. Some of the questions were suggested by young people themselves. No doubt important themes have been left out: baptism, the Trinity, the Creed, the Commandments, miracles, social justice, and many others. There may be another occasion for these.

A glance through the list of contents will give the reader the menu. It falls into three different parts: making sense of God's existence; issues of living the Christian life; more theological questions. In other words – approaching faith, living faith, and understanding faith. (Some of the material in the first section draws on a series of articles I wrote for *The Sacred Heart Messenger* in 1994.)

While writing these pages I found myself coming back again and again to a similar 'strategy' in trying to do justice to these themes. It involves saying: beware of trying to understand this in a superficial way – we are talking about something profound, something about God. Don't expect that you can always have answers within the bounds of common sense: our so-called common sense can be full of blinkers and blockages. Because of this we condemn ourselves to inadequate answers to key questions about the gift at the core of life. I hope in this book to suggest more adequate answers than can be found through common sense.

In John's Gospel there is a recurring gap between Jesus and many of his audience. He is often communicating on one level but they are caught on a level that condemns them to misunderstand him. The classic example is the woman at the well (in chapter 4) who is offered 'living water' and replies 'you have no bucket – how would you get this water?' A literal quotation! And a perfect example of the clash between common sense – like arguing about religion in a pub – and the wavelength required to appreciate what this reality called faith is all about.

So the invitation is to put down your 'bucket' as you read this book. Indeed it is something I have frequently had to do in writing these short responses to large questions. Each of them is a whole world of richness and the temptation is to approach them in a spirit of mere argument. Getting rid of the bucket does not mean abandoning intelligent searching but doing it in a spirit of reverence and openness to a Person at the centre of all this story of God. It is fascinating that at the end of her conversation with Jesus the woman of Samaria 'put down her water-jar'. It symbolises beautifully that she had found a different kind of water.

Much of this book is devoted to clarifying our understanding of faith. But faith is more than just finding that living water. What did the Samaritan woman do with the rest of her life? We do not know, but surely that meeting marked a revolution in all her ways of seeing *and* acting. Indeed, Jesus made fun of people who go around saying 'Lord, Lord', but do not 'do' what is at the core of faith.

In a similar vein, I remember a conversation with Canadian writer Northrop Frye. At one point he said something simple but challenging that has stayed with me ever since: 'You don't believe what you say you believe, but only what you live'.

These pages cannot teach anyone how to live. That would be too much. And yet the goal of all this talk about faith is to prepare the way of the Lord, who can then liberate us for the adventure of living differently.

Michael Paul Gallagher

PART I

APPROACHING FAITH

Making Sense of
God's Existence

1

Some people seem to believe in a cosy God and others in a fearful one. Who is God really?

Over the years I have spent a good deal of time with people who say they cannot believe in God. As I listen, a question I sometimes ask myself is 'which God?' And quite often, after hearing their description of not believing, I find myself saying to them: 'But I don't believe in that God either'.

Nearly everybody suffers from negative pictures of God which lurk in the imagination. Even theologians, who may have a deep understanding of the things of God, can find that their feelings have not caught up with their ideas.

Let me describe the situation of one young man, whose faith was cramped by his image of God. Daniel went through a period of distance from faith and practice in his mid-teens. Then, quite suddenly, when he was about twenty he decided that his scattered life-style was leading nowhere. Spontaneity and 'hanging loose' were all very fine at fifteen, but to stay too long in that groove would be immature. He realised that he wanted to 'settle down', to find 'anchors', and to live a more 'generous life'.

So Daniel went back to the sacraments and found the whole area of Christian values more central to his life than ever before. He 'needed guidelines', he said, and in the old practices that he had abandoned as 'empty and boring', he now found surprising support. But one day he came to me with an unusual request. 'I've more or less sorted out my behaviour', he said, but 'I don't think I'm really a Christian'. What he meant by this was quite simple: he had returned to a certain obedience to Christian ethics, but he still found himself with little or no sense of Jesus Christ.

As we talked this over, it became clear that, without realising it, Daniel had 'regressed' to a strand of his earlier childhood religion, when a certain external obedience had been strong and even central. At the age of seven or eight a child can be very rigid in this area: just think of how strict they are about keeping the rules of a game.

But at twenty Daniel's image of God was still mainly a 'Behaviour Boss', who expected him to improve his conduct and who watched this process from a distance – like a superintendent in an examination hall. He told me: 'Unless I have some other sense of God, this whole journey is too lonely'. Dead on, as Daniel himself might say. The journey of faith was never meant to be such a lonely and uphill struggle of will-power. At the heart of the gospel is the person of Jesus who says exactly the opposite: Remain in me, with me in you, and you will bear much fruit… without me you can do nothing (John 15:5).

I am convinced that many people get stuck at this stage of development. They experience religion mainly as a matter of norms and conduct, and they miss the invitation to a personal relationship with Christ that is at the heart of it all.

How can you tell that some distorted image of God is present? One sign is when the words 'God loves you' suggest only a distant and vague truth. As an older woman once said to me (and she was far from being an 'unbeliever'): 'God loves everyone but …(she paused) I don't know about me'. 'You mean God does not love *you?*' 'No, I'm sure he does but I've never really known it.' That is the point. There is a threshold between a God-who-is-theory and a God-who-becomes-personal. Cardinal Newman called it the difference between 'notional assent' and 'real assent'. And the 'God' rejected by some unbelievers is a notional picture of the wrong god!

There are other signs of sub-Christian gods: where God is more distant and controlling than close by and 'on my side'; where avoiding breaking God's law takes centre stage, at the expense of any sense of God's compassion for my struggles; where forgiveness is conditional on my 'pulling up my socks'; where

God is a super-power who sometimes works magic for us, or a moody monarch who might not be in good humour today, or a judge with indigestion after lunch, who could hand down a tough sentence out of grumpiness.

All these false images occur because of overly human and pessimistic pictures of law and fear. In the New Testament St Paul was the great rebel against a religion that remained on the level of mere legalism. St John was equally strong: 'In love there is no room for fear' (1 John 4:18). If people get stuck with their childhood sense of obedience and punishment, then their God can become unbelievable when they are adults.

In the last few years there have been complaints that the younger generation have no genuine 'fear of God', that they tend to believe in a softy God, a mister-nice-guy-in-the-sky. No doubt there is truth in that: some have an image of a totally permissive God. They confuse God's constant forgiveness of those who try to turn away from their selfishness with an 'anything-goes' kind of God. But I think the main danger still lies in the opposite direction: even for those brought up in the less strict times of the 1970s and after, the most frequent false image of God is often too moral, too demanding, too impersonal and too distant. This is what Daniel's God was like, with the result was that he himself felt continually under a cloud and incapable of good.

In my book *Free to Believe* I had a chapter on false images of God; readers have told me they were helped (and amused) by a true story I told there about a priest making a personal retreat, who remarked to me on the first day, 'I think God should give me a good kick.' When he repeated exactly the same thing the following day, I asked him, 'Would Jesus give you a good kick?' 'Oh no', was his immediate and even shocked reply. 'So Jesus is not God', I said. And he laughed, embarrassed to discover his heresy of images!

2   *Over a few drinks recently some friends had a good argument about the existence of God but I'm not sure that anybody convinced anyone else. Is it just a matter of accepting it?*

As Shakespeare says in *Hamlet,* 'the readiness is all'. And that question of readiness is a key to talking about anything important in life – love, faith, death, suffering, why we are here. Sometimes we try to ask questions about God 'from the outside', without really being in touch with our hungers. And so the whole thing becomes a word-game, a clever argument – something that doesn't reach the heart. If I remain distant in this way, I will never find God. If I drift on the surface of things, I can block God from finding me. Many arguments about whether or not 'God exists' – as a mere fact 'out there' – can be beside the point. Unless it's a burning question, not just a surface one, the wavelength is wrong. I can keep myself shielded from the hungers within me and then from the surprise that is called Revelation. Christian faith is born from that surprise of being reached out to by God in Jesus Christ.

Is that gift of Revelation the only road to faith? Surely there are avenues of questioning about God that do not go beyond what we can work out for ourselves. Yes, this is true (and I look at some of these later). But these paths of inquiry are preparations for what is central – the listening to Christ that answers the long-ing of each person.

Any kind of questioning about the existence of God needs a special spirit of reverence. Since we are tackling a question that touches everything about us and our lives, unless our approach is filled with a kind of wonder, it will stay superficial. The famous philosopher, Jacques Maritain, used to insist that any argument about the existence of God had to start from a sense of amaze-ment that I am here at all. In his opinion, waking up to the surprise of my own existence is a beginning and basis for all the more worked-out reasonings about God. Therefore I can be on the wrong wavelength in my search unless I sense something of the strangeness of my being alive at all.

Psalm 139 has the simple prayer: 'I thank you for the wonder of myself'. To nourish that attitude before your very existence, try this little exercise. If you give it a little time, it can awaken the personal awe that Maritain had in mind. Close your eyes and imagine the same place where you are reading this as it was one hundred years ago – before you were ever thought of. It is probable that the building that you are in was not there at all. Stay with this idea, trying to picture for yourself the scene as it might have been then. Next, change the focus, and try to imagine what the same place will be like one hundred years in the future – when you will not be here either! Will someone else be here? Will there be another building? What might it look like? Finally, come back to now, and to yourself here. Rest with the simple awareness of being alive and present in this world. If you wish, make some prayer of gratitude for your life, knowing that it is both short and special: 'I thank you for the wonder of myself'.

An exercise like that – and please don't rush it – can help to get in touch with what Maritain called an 'intuition of existence'. Then the existence of God is no longer a mere problem, but an overwhelming question, a mystery embracing us. You can't stand outside it as a cold observer. Where you stand influences what you see – and this is true of many things, even God.

3   *My father says he was 'taught' clear proofs for the existence of God but he forgets what they are! Do they still hold?*

Many people who had a Catholic secondary education before the mid-1960s would have studied a book commonly referred to as Sheehan's *Apologetics*. I can still recall the satisfaction of having proved the existence of God so conclusively. How stupid atheists were not to see something so obvious!

But that was a world ago. Now those old arguments are seen to be, not entirely false, but too cut off from human reality. In practice they convinced nobody who did not *want* to be convinced. The existence of God is not something that can be solved by the detached mind, like someone investigating the presence of salt on the moon. The question about God is always a question about humanity, about who we are ultimately. So it entails not only 'objective' thinking but a personal decision.

And yet objective thinking has a role. One ancient line of argument started from our existence here in this world. It stressed that there is a magnificent order in everything, pointing to some purpose, ultimately to some creator. For instance, we know more about the human brain today than was known in Sheehan's time: we know that it is perhaps the most complex single object in the universe. We can study it in all sorts of ways but then we come up against another question: Why? The cosmos itself is vaster than we ever imagined and, as Einstein remarked, 'the eternal mystery of the world is its *comprehensibility*'. And behind this order, this comprehensibility? Scientists today are much less hostile to the notion of mystery than they were a hundred years ago, when a mechanical model tried to account for everything. Nowadays the question of God is not despised because our knowledge is so much more complex.

There is another side to all this: that older approach – of cold reason – was much influenced by the French philosopher Descartes, whose starting point was the statement: 'I think, therefore I am'. He seemed to imply that we do our thinking in total isolation, but is this true? The best criticism of Descartes is also the simplest: he should have said, 'I think, therefore *we* are' (see Question 16). We learn to talk and to think only from others. To forget the crucial role of family and of community is to imagine that everyone has to work out the meaning of life from scratch and alone.

A similar mistake is often made in relation to religious faith. Lonely thinking is not enough. Instead it is a matter of trusting God, which in practice becomes more possible by trusting the goodness of others. The presence of believing friends can help me find faith. The non-support of society can block the possibility of faith. Even if these new pressures can make a faith decision harder today, perhaps they also make it more honest.

Descartes (and Sheehan) underestimated the relevance of all this for faith – the impact of society or of changing culture on the possibility of making a faith decision. They avoided the decision element in faith. They saw it as some kind of pure truth, and this narrowness proved dangerous in ways. Their detached logic often produced a detached, and therefore, irrelevant God, not the God of Christian revelation.

Further back than Descartes, St Thomas Aquinas insisted that faith differs from ordinary knowing, because it entails a mixture of understanding and deciding. Thinking takes us only part of the way towards faith: God will always remain beyond any human knowing. We come up against mystery, which means something too rich for our usual understanding.

In all this journey of thinking our way towards faith, a stage comes when many pieces of evidence point towards the reality of God, and when the possibility of believing becomes attractive. But who is this God? When I realise that the only God worth believing in is a God of love and of relationship, a new logic takes over. On the balance of the evidence, my mind is satisfied that I ought to believe. Humanly, I want to believe: it is in tune with my heart's desires. But more deeply and personally, I find myself invited to believe – to trust the prompting of the Spirit within me. In this way a decision to believe becomes possible, and this overcomes what is lacking as external 'proof'.

Of course this decision is not always so easily reached. Today's culture and life-styles can eclipse the attractiveness of God. The human failures of the Church can overshadow a lot of the good things that Church people do. Since faith is a free choice, various hurts of life can get in the way at this point, where we stand at an important transition between thinking *about* God and surrendering to the revelation *of* God.

The great Canadian theologian, Bernard Lonergan, described faith as 'the knowledge born from love'. When two people move towards being in love with one another, they judge things differently. Sheehan and Descartes, and many people who stick to stern logic, might dismiss all this as soft and woolly. But in fact all the deeper realities of life go beyond proofs and external reasoning. They involve decisions, trust, discernment of a more delicate kind – in a logic of love.

We can give many reasons for God's existence, all of which are helpful in their own way. But they never add up to faith. Perhaps faith can be described as 'a yes to a yes': God says yes to us in Jesus Christ, and we respond with a hesitant but lived yes that is called faith. That response involves a decision of saying yes to Someone, who has already said the yes of love to us. Our yes is not a matter of pure reason. It is rooted in our whole attitude to life.

Quite simply, when I try to love others, I am more ready to understand God's love, to which I say yes in faith. Cardinal Newman put it boldly: 'We believe because we love'. Or, as Jesus once said: 'Whoever *does* the truth comes into the light'. Once more, the emphasis falls on what we really live, not on the cleverness of our reasoning.

Perhaps that last and central point can be summed up in another variant on Descartes: 'We love, therefore You are'.

4

Do we believe in God simply because we want to? Or are there good reasons that can make sense today?

The desire for God is written in the heart of humanity. This is the first sentence of the first chapter of the *Catechism of the Catholic Church.* It goes on to list three 'roads that lead to knowing God'. Firstly, there is the longing for happiness and for the infinite in each person. Secondly, everyone has a sense of moral good, which we each experience in the exercise of our freedom. And, thirdly, experience of truth and beauty opens us out beyond ourselves. I would describe these three roads as the way of desire, the way of conscience, and the way of wonder. These are not 'proofs' for God in a scientific sense, but they are certainly pointers that make us think.

Let us tease out the first of these three approaches to belief in God – the 'way of desire'. Most people know something of the story of St Augustine, who spent years searching for God, and going through a good deal of emotional turmoil and resistance. On the first page of his *Confessions* comes the famous sentence that 'our hearts are restless' until they find peace in God. The hunger is deep inside everyone, but some people never get in touch with it, because a more external restlessness takes over, and pressures of many kinds can keep them nervously on the move.

When did you last really sit down and listen to your own hopes? If you get in touch with your deepest self, you find a powerful longing for something or someone beyond yourself. In Saul Bellow's novel, *Henderson the Rain King,* the central character is both rich and successful but a voice inside him keeps saying 'I want, I want'. A hunger like that can be fulfilled by the love of another person. But there is more to it. It invites us beyond human hopes towards the possibility of God.

Some people would dismiss this line of thinking as 'wish fulfilment', or 'projection', or 'pie in the sky'. They suspect it of being a childish fantasy: we simply imagine a God who will satisfy all our desires, fill in what is missing in life and relieve us of human responsibility for this world.

But there is a flaw in this argument. It views our desire for God as rooted in weakness or in a sense of inadequacy. Augustine's restlessness involved a sense of something missing, but it was not just a negative experience. It was a positive desire. Something was lacking in his life, and he knew it. But this sense of something not yet found awoke him to a fullness that he was meant to have.

'Our biggest obstacle to believing in God', writes the theologian Sebastian Moore, 'is our innate distrust of happiness. This is a disbelief in our own goodness.' He asks us to reflect on moments that give us a 'passionate sense of our worth'. It is not just moments of failure that point us towards God, but also the times when the joy of life puts us in tune with our deepest desire.

There are two messages here for those who find belief in God difficult. Firstly, it takes time: Augustine was struggling for years before he could say 'yes' to faith and realise that God had been waiting for him all those years.

Secondly, it means being in touch with your own experience: 'Cast your net into the depths' is Jesus' invitation at one moment in the gospel (Luke 5:4). Make sure you don't remain just on the surface of your experience.

5 *As I move out of my teens, I am not too happy with my old ways of acting. Could this be a message from God?*

I'LL ANSWER with a life story. Silvano is an Italian student in his mid-twenties who began to take his religious faith seriously only a few years ago. He had a traditional Catholic upbringing but drifted from it during his teenage years. His 'return' to the faith came about because he found himself forced into a crisis of choice. He got into contact with some dangerous people, who offered him the possibility of quick but dishonest money. Initially he flirted with the idea of accepting. It would have solved a few of his problems.

However, he asked for some time to think about it, and this proved to be one of the turning-points of his life. He asked himself: if I take this road, what does it mean for my whole future? The answer frightened him. For the first time as an adult, he woke up to the fact that the quality of his life depended on his own decisions. He had been drifting a lot, he realised. But now he knew that he would be damaging something for good if he took the easy option. This decision was the first major choice of his life. At the same time, and unexpectedly for him, he saw that he needed to 'sort himself out' religiously. This moral decision had opened him up to a whole host of new questions. What was he living for? Where was God in all this? – if there was a God.

So Silvano came to see that this experience of conscience was, at least for him, an indirect experience of God. Later he explained his discovery like this:

> At a certain point I saw that I could not be true to myself if I took this money. Once I recognised that, the decision was made. There was really no struggle, once I admitted to myself that this call of conscience was right. To my surprise

this 'voice' was not a bossy one. It was more like hearing music perfectly in tune. And this serenity made me realise that following my conscience was a way of meeting God. God was not only saving me from a false move, but was showing me how I could return to faith again. It would be a new relationship, no longer a childhood one. I knew that God was Someone who wanted to reach me, and this God was way beyond the behaviour zone, even though it was a crisis over behaviour that opened my eyes.

That hardly needs much comment. Perhaps many a young person loses touch with faith and goes through a period of drifting and confusion. But quite often this period of immediacy runs into a rut. It can become empty and boring or, as in Silvano's case, it can be jolted into new questioning, and even towards new faith in God.

This road to faith was not first discovered by Silvano! Perhaps of all the great Christian thinkers, it was Cardinal Newman who most explored conscience and wonder as avenues towards God. He said, 'if I am asked why I believe in a God, I answer that it is because I believe in myself', and he goes on to say that his deepest experiences of self drew him to believe in One 'who lives as a Personal, All-seeing, All-judging Being in my conscience'. Writing in the last century, with all its explosion of new knowledge in the field of science, Newman was a little sceptical of the older ways of proving God's existence. He was not convinced by approaches that started from the 'phenomena of the physical world, taken by themselves'. Indeed, he is very modern in his preference for a more psychological approach, starting from what he calls 'inward experience'. And he adds, 'conscience is nearer to me than any other means of knowledge'.

Silvano does not use the same language, and yet he too came to believe in himself, as Newman would say. He understood that the drama of that first important choice would shape his whole life. Something deep and precious was at stake. He glimpsed his own personal value, and saw how it was in danger. But there were other echoes of Newman. Silvano heard God, so to speak, through his conscience and his wondering. The whole tussle became something larger than a human choice. It was not just a matter of avoiding evil. It was a call to responsibility, goodness and commitment. It became an encounter with God as Companion within the very adventure of being human.

In 1833, while still fairly young, Newman had written a poem entitled 'Sensitiveness' about this kind of transition from a morality of right-and-wrong to a recognition of a personal God. His first stage was negative:

> Time was, I shrank from what was right
> From fear of what was wrong.

But this experience of anxious conscience gave way to another stage of realising that he was not alone:

> So, when my Saviour calls, I rise,
> And calmly do my best;
> Leaving to Him, with silent eyes
> Of hope and fear, the rest.

Why is life so cruel if God is love?

This is certainly the hardest question of all to answer rationally. The theologian Karl Rahner admitted that the various intellectual objections to God seem easy compared with the desolations of existence when they strike. Through the centuries people have agonised over the question: if God is good and powerful, why is there such terrible suffering? And the best answers offer variations on one humble truth: we do not know, there is no neat answer. Or, as French dramatist Paul Claudel once wrote: 'God did not come to take away our suffering, nor to explain it; Jesus came to fill it with his presence.'

When someone is in the midst of a crisis of personal pain, the urge to give an answer can be unworthy of the agony they are going through. Silence is best, a silent presence of sharing the burden. But there are calmer moments when some thoughts and ideas can help. At least they can rid us of a few false notions and cast some limited light. I can think of four avenues of reflection that are worthwhile, and I outline them with deliberate brevity.

1. God's power does not mean magic interference in our world. Some theologians would say that God's only omnipotence is love.
2. God does not cause evil, but for some reason permits it. Or better still, God suffers with us.
3. Sometimes suffering can be fruitful. Think of King Lear coming through pride and madness into a humble serenity and even a glimpse of redemption.
4. A possible side-effect of suffering is to purify sub-Christian images of a God who is distant, untouched by our pain, or who is punishing us for some wrong. 'I missed Mass that Sunday

and my child was knocked down': in moments of panic that kind of superstition is not far from any of us. Our imagination takes a long time to catch up with our understanding.

Of course such comments may be quite useless to the person actually suffering. They can be like Job's 'comforters', those friends who only added to his frustration with their efforts to explain everything.

Indeed, that famous story from the Bible remains one of the extraordinary expressions of all time on the question of God and suffering. When Job's three visitors offer theological chatter about suffering as a punishment for guilt, he attacks these easy explanations as 'whitewash' and as the 'dusty answers' of quack doctors! (13:4,11). The book is full of Job's anger and rebellion: he comes to hate his own life and feels God to be deaf and 'cruel' (30:21). He demands a meeting with God but he does not 'curse' God, in the sense of rejecting divine goodness. And when God eventually comes to meet Job, it is not to solve the question of suffering in a rational way. Instead Job gets a glimpse of how different everything looks from God's perspective: just as all images fall short of God's mystery, so too the desire to explain is doomed to failure.

In this masterpiece of the Old Testament, suffering is seen as a real challenge to faith, especially to notions of God that remain immature or legalistic. Our anger and God's silence clash in the darkness that is suffering – and that is part of every life sooner or later. But through all the turmoil, like Job we may emerge into a trusting belief that God wants only to create life, even out of the chaos of suffering.

Something of that message was part of the experience of C. S. Lewis, the convert atheist who became a celebrated lay theologian in the Anglican Church. The film *Shadowlands* brought his own drama of suffering to a large public.

Anyone who has seen it will remember how Anthony Hopkins,

playing the part of Lewis, lectured on the question of suffering and how to reconcile it with the goodness of God. In ringing and confident tones he proclaimed how pain could be understood as God's 'megaphone to rouse a deaf world': 'God whispers to us in our pleasures, speaks in our conscience, but shouts in our pains'. Lewis, at this stage of his life, viewed suffering as having a 'remedial' purpose, shattering our illusion of self-sufficiency and forcing us to become aware of our need for God and for redemption.

This was a lucid, if somewhat stern and puritan interpretation of God and of suffering. But the film went on to show how these theories crumbled as a result of the death of his young wife after only three years of happy marriage. Her battle with cancer and then the aftermath of her death revealed the weakness of his fine words: their definite tone now seemed hollow beside the reality of suffering. Lewis found himself shattered in ways that his explanations had never envisaged.

He began to keep a diary of his many changing moods, and (something not shown in the film) over several months he filled four notebooks which he eventually published without (at that time) using his own name: it was called *A Grief Observed*. The early sections voiced a good deal of anger. There was a sense that God had slammed a door in his face. And the question arose as to which God he still believed in – since God seemed like a Cosmic Sadist, leading us up the garden path of hope, but in fact 'preparing the next torture'. Lewis wrote those bitter words one night, and then the next day added that it was 'a yell rather than a thought'. But the yells at this stage of his mourning were honest and necessary. In his memorable words, 'it doesn't really matter whether you grip the arms of the dentist's chair or let your hands lie in your lap. The drill drills on.'

The later notebooks speak of unexpected clearings in the forest. 'The less I mourn her the nearer I seem to her'; because one cannot see properly with eyes 'blurred with tears'. God's door did not seem bolted shut any more, and Lewis asked himself whether perhaps he himself had slammed it. 'I need Christ', he writes, 'not something that resembles Him'. As with Job, God does not answer and yet seems to have been present, unrecognised in all the darkness: it was 'like a silent, certainly not uncompassionate, gaze. As though He shook His head not in refusal but waiving the question. Like, 'Peace, child; you don't understand'.

But the gospels have a more powerful light to offer. We can try to say: 'If you look at the Crucifix, you see the love of God suffering *our human* cruelty – and overcoming it forever in the Resurrection.' Once again we are beyond logic and arguments. We are in the logic of love, a love that takes on suffering. In this spirit there is a moment from the Jewish novelist Elie Wiesel that, without mentioning Christ, hints at what is an 'answer' to suffering. He evokes one of the horrors of the Auschwitz concentration camp, the public hanging of a child together with two adults. As the chairs were kicked from under each of them, a voice said, 'Where is God now?' 'And I heard a voice within me answer him: 'Where is He? Here He is – He is hanging here on this gallows.'

7   *Why is the existence of God such a problem for us?*
Surely any 'decent' God would do a better job of
communication, and not leave us so much in the
dark, wondering?

Let me start with a little fantasy. Think of a deaf person wandering into a concert hall while players in an orchestra are warming up for a rehearsal. He or she sees violinists pulling their bows against their instruments, stopping and starting again, or trombonists pulling a piece of brass in and out, or a drummer hitting a circle of skin and twisting knobs, and so on. And let's imagine that the deaf person has never even heard of music.

At first this variety of activity might be fascinating. But a point comes when the excitement doesn't satisfy any more. What on earth is going on? What the deaf person sees seems mad. They're all doing their own thing. Without order. And without any sound.

Then in comes the conductor to begin the rehearsal. People stop their individual activity, and the deaf person sees the conductor raise a baton. The players now move in the same way as before but with a new unity. Following the baton. Our deaf friend might guess that there is some kind of order, even though it is impossible to hear it. What seemed crazy now has some pattern, even though it does not make full sense.

Suppose, for the sake of the story, that into that concert hall comes an extraordinary ear specialist, who has invented a cure for this kind of deafness. It is, let's say, a little ear-plug with electrodes that immediately stimulates into life the paralysed capacity to hear. And let us imagine that the doctor gives this marvellous cure to the deaf person. What a transformation! For the first time ever he or she is overwhelmed with sound, with a torrent of music, seeing all these movements of the musicians as making perfect sense, perfect harmony. Seeing and hearing come together, and at last everything has meaning.

Let's suppose that the great specialist can explain all this. The players are not just making beautiful sounds. This is a symphony by Beethoven. He composed all this beauty.

What does that little parable suggest? Perhaps the reader should not immediately read the next paragraph, but rather pause and think a bit. What might be the connection between this story and the question asked about God? In fact there is no single, correct interpretation: what I will say is one way of reading it, but not the only one.

The little parable has four acts: mere happenings, a glimpse of order, a fuller meaning, a gift of knowing.

At first it all seems to be just one thing after another, with no connection. Even our experience of ourselves is largely scattered, all bits and pieces. Like all these players doing fragmented things. One thing happens after another. We can live that way for years, even happily. Being young means, perhaps in part, being contented with the adventure of events just happening, without any great need to make sense of them. Then a time comes when living for the moment is no longer enough. What does it all mean? Is it all simply empty? Does anything matter?

Even asking those questions is asking for light, for the entry of the conductor, for insight. I discover that I can make some sense of my life. I look around and glimpse some kind of order – in the universe itself, in my own heart. Some things begin to come together. My own mind and heart are beginning to make sense of what seemed chaotic. Yes, life has some meaning, I think, but how can I be sure? What I glimpse is very shaky. Watching the conductor but being deaf, I see only the possibility of pattern. I have not arrived.

The specialist is the one who liberates me to hear. This is a kind of salvation. It is the role of Christ, who comes to heal us for seeing and hearing: the gospels are full of such moments.

But the gospel is more than a story of a healer and preacher. It is about who Christ is, and about his telling us of the Father and the Spirit. Christ comes to show us the humanity of God. Through him we know the full story of life as a love story. Finding out about the creative genius of Beethoven is only a distant parallel.

Perhaps all this is a way of questioning the initial question. Are we so much in the dark after all? Even on our own, with the help of our mind (the conductor) we can begin to see some pattern. For the first two acts we seem to be on our own. But then there comes a change, a meeting point between our searching and God's answer in Christ. The adventure of faith is a bit like that.

8   *What do we mean by 'faith'?*

One cynical answer runs: believing incredible theories, because they don't make too much difference in this life but they might help in the next!

I'd like to demolish that answer bit by bit; not just for the sake of argument, but because it's sad that something as important as faith is so often thought of in such a childish way.

Let's take the negative side first – the need to get rid of wrong impressions.

1   It's much more than theory: it's either about a God who loves us, and reaches out to help us realise that, or it's rubbish.

2.   It's not simply a matter of 'beliefs', or some strange ideas that you accept: it's rooted in a whole attitude towards yourself and life.

3.   It's far from stupid or incredible: there are very good reasons for believing in God even though they never add up to a watertight 'proof' – which would not be 'faith'.

4.   If it doesn't make any difference, then it's not the passionate faith of the Bible: from the prophets to Jesus there is a long battle on two fronts against merely external religion and costly struggle – God is trying to change our hearts so that we can heal this wounded world.

5   Jesus Christ promises us 'fullness of life', but it's not just after death: it involves sharing his journey now as well.

Positively, faith means a certain disposition – a 'recognising attitude'. We can go through life without noticing things. Or at least we can get into certain moods when we are insensitive to people around. We rush past them, not noticing their pain or even their joys. When Jesus said that unless you become as a child, you will not enter the Kingdom, he was talking about this level of disposition. Without some wonder or some sensitivity, the whole world of human love becomes impossible. And faith is about love.

Which brings me to the other side of faith: God's side, so to speak. Faith is not just about God's existence, but about who God is for us, or, better, who God wants to be for us. Notice the language – 'wants' and 'for us'. In other words, it's about a desire and a relationship. God's desire to have a relationship with you and with me! Faith without this core is not Christian faith.

Here is the simplest definition of faith that I can imagine: it is a yes to a yes. God says yes to us in Christ, a yes of love. Not softy love but tough and total and steady. And we say a more unsteady yes back – unsteady because we do not see God in this life.

And a marvellous image can accompany that simplest of definitions. In the last lecture of his life, the great theologian Hans Urs von Balthasar spoke of faith, and used a parallel that he had written about many times before. If you want to understand faith, ponder the first smile of a new-born infant. In fact the first real smile does not usually happen until into the second month. Balthasar talked about it as a first act of freedom, born from being loved by the mother. When the first smile comes, what is it saying? (Obviously not in words – 'infant' comes from the Latin for speechless.) Long before verbal communication, the first smile is saying something like: 'I recognise that I am loved'. And that is the core of Christian faith. We recognise a gift, a yes, a relationship started by God. Long before our unsteady 'yes', the 'yes' of God surrounded us like a mother's love.

Or, as already mentioned, Bernard Lonergan sees faith as 'a knowledge born from love'.

PART II

LIVING FAITH

Living the Christian Life

9

Why do you think believing in God is more diffi-cult for the younger generation than for our parents?

I'm sure you could answer this better yourself – from your own experience of the differences in attitude between you and your parents. All I can offer is a few suggestions from someone who himself grew up before all the major changes happened in Church and world.

Let's start with three quick but significant examples. My childhood was pre-television! That arrived gradually during my teens. My schooling was the old-fashioned kind of do-what-you-are-told or else the stick or the leather came into action. My sense of the Church was shared with everyone around me: in the village where I grew up, not going to Mass on Sunday was practically unknown for Catholics. In short, a simpler world, a more ordered or obedient world, and a more unified world. You might describe it more critically as too protected, ruled by fear and very con-formist. Yes, perhaps, but there was a certain rootedness and secu-rity in spite of the warts.

That's an important background for this question about diffi-culty regarding faith. The whole context is radically changed. Your parents had social supports for becoming and remaining believers that have practically disappeared nowadays. You could say that your parents' generation did not have to make a major religious decision: they more or less inherited faith from their own parents and grandparents. But your generation can't inherit faith so smoothly. Perhaps you 'inherit' instead a kind of confu-sion or doubt, not from your parents but from the pressures around you. The result is that you can only become mature believers against the tide. And that is only possible with the help of a whole series of growth points touched on elsewhere in these pages: community, a sense of Christ, prayer, options for self-giving, and so on.

'There's a whole new culture'. This word 'culture' has come into fashion to explain something important. Even the word itself has shifted its meaning. It used to mean things like literature and classical music, the creative or artistic side of how we human beings 'cultivate' ourselves, just as a farmer cultivates the earth. But today a second meaning is becoming the dominant one. Pope John Paul II talks about culture as 'everything that shapes the human person and the community in which we live'. It means a way of life that seems natural (but in fact may be quite unnatural).

Why mention all this? We are 'shaped' by all this world around us. There have been enormous changes in this area since your parents were young themselves. And, most of all, this new culture can have little room for God or for Church or even for searching. Reading a book like this is a counter-cultural activity!

Don't get me wrong on this. I'm not saying that the world has gone to the dogs and there is nothing good about the culture around us today. There are positive values of freedom and honesty and a sense of justice. There is a search for genuine friendship and generosity. But the new culture can also be superficial: it produces trends in clothes, music and attitudes, and can have an irrational hostility towards institutions. So we need to have a few healthy suspicions about this ocean of influences in which we swim.

I have given you two main answers so far, both of which echo Christ's parable about the sower. For you the supports for faith are less numerous and less available than for your parents. One result of this is that you can find yourselves lacking 'roots', as the parable puts it. Secondly, there are forces around that can cause a lack of hunger for the vision of faith: the parable talked about the 'birds of the air' that take away the seed before it has even had a

38

chance to sink into the earth. Religion is not very 'interesting' for the dominant culture, except as a source of controversy. That parable also spoke of the little plant of faith being 'choked' by weeds, and it interpreted the weeds as the distractions of life, the busyness with external things. The life-styles that are sold to your generation (and 'sold' or 'marketed' are apt words) aim at keeping you on the move. They are not interested in stillness or quiet moments for the heart.

Of course 'culture' is not exactly the same as 'society', which relates more to the external structures that surround us. 'Culture' includes all sorts of values and meanings and symbols which need not be simply external. Perhaps cultural change is less rapid than social change. For example, in Ireland there was a decade of huge social change in the 1960s: more money, even an economic boom, television, a big movement from rural areas to towns and cities. But these are external influences. Culture is a matter of deeper attitudes and assumptions.

In this light, perhaps you are not as different from your parents as you think. Society has changed a lot. Culture is also changing but not so rapidly. The externals of religious practice that were so central for your parents in their youth are simply not central for you. But something else is central: a search for meaning, for honesty, for a genuine basis for life. And this is the 'cultural' side of things, which I think you share with your parents. There are problems about the 'language of faith', but I don't really believe that many people have a 'crisis of faith' itself. The longing for God remains. The sense of Christ (even if often vague) is an anchor for many people of your generation. A culture of surface distractions may be invading people's hearts: everyone complains about television or noise, even as they immerse themselves in them. But if roots are deep, perhaps the damage is only superficial. Not that many people are taken in by all that silliness, to the extent of not experiencing hungers and hopes for the presence of God in their lives. I am always surprised by the surveys that show how many people pray personally a few times a week (even if they don't go to church on Sunday).

Your approach to the externals of religion which, by the way, are also important – don't get me wrong (see Question 11 on Church) – is different from that of your parents. But perhaps you share with them something more fundamental: the hunch that God is real and that somehow it is possible to be in living contact with that great Love.

10 *Are we really meant to be happy?*

The poet Yeats said once that we have not grown up fully until we realise that life is tragic. Another famous twentieth-century writer, the Australian Patrick White, adds that Christianity becomes soft and sugary when it forgets the darker sides of existence. But I still want to answer yes to this question, and not simply because there is another happiness awaiting us beyond this life (I explore this in Question 25). I believe that our deepest human happiness can survive even suffering or moments of tragedy. It is not a matter of always feeling on top of the world. It can be a very struggling kind of happiness.

Think of the simple but powerful words of the marriage ceremony: 'I take you "for better or worse".' It claims that this couple trust one another so much that they can face the mixture together, hoping that they can build – overall – an adventure of happiness. Pause on that last bit. 'Overall' doesn't mean steady moods and bubbling good form every day, it sometimes means pain and confusion. 'Build' means that happiness does not just 'happen', no, it is an adventure of ups and downs to be worked at *together*. Then a certain strong happiness comes quietly as a by-product, not as something sought in itself. There is a popular image of happiness as being like a butterfly: chase it and you will not catch it, but sit quietly and it might come to rest on your shoulder.

What is true for a married couple is true for all of us. We are meant to be happy, but our happiness depends a great deal on learning to trust and to love. Not everyone has an equal start. Some people are more blessed than others – in the circumstances that shape them, especially in the family relationships that create a whole attitude towards life. An American survey interviewed a selection of contented people in an attempt to identify some common denominator, and ended up coining the word 'good-finder'. These happy people all had a gift or a basic attitude that allowed them to discover good even when things were difficult. They were more than incurable optimists. Instead they had learnt to trust life, to find goodness in themselves and in others, and to know that darkness need not damage and will not last.

But happiness is not just psychological. In the light of Christian faith, it is a promise from God, for this life and beyond. The answer of Jesus might be: Yes, you are meant to be happy but along a road that is not always easy, a road I walked myself. Or remember some words from the gospels: 'I have come that they may have life and have it to the full' (John 10:10); let 'my own joy be in you and your joy be complete' (John 15:11).

Any Christian answer to this question must mention the Beatitudes. Think of them as autobiographical, as if Jesus is speaking of his own secret formula for being happy. It involves a whole series of attitudes that he lived: being aware of his inner poverty and keeping his heart pure, being gentle and forgiving, feeling for those in pain and creating peace around him, wanting to heal the injustices of this world. (See Matthew 5:3-10) These are not 'other-worldly' forms of happiness. They start here. They can be verified. You will be much happier being compassionate than being hard, trying to help others than just being 'out for yourself' and so on.

But Jesus links these heart-options with promises of sharing God's fuller happiness. And he even tells us, 'happy are those who are persecuted for the cause of right, for theirs is the kingdom of heaven'. Throughout the ages many philosophers agreed that we all want to be happy. They saw that it was connected with how we choose to live, and therefore it means seeing through false forms of short-lived happiness. But no philosopher made promises like those of Jesus, and no philosopher ever included suffering 'on my account' as a source of happiness. The Christian picture is much bigger.

So, yes, we are meant to be happy, but it's sometimes a steep road.

11 *I have my own kind of faith in Christ. What's so important about the Church?*

This is a burning question for people today. It is not only a question of the hurt and anger caused by various scandals. It is a deeper issue of a certain distrust of institutions and of all forms of authority. The social conscience of the 1960s has given way to a different mood, where the individual life seems more private than before. Some commentators talk of post-modernity, meaning that we have lost hope in our capacity to change the world and we retreat into the 'self'. Whatever the explanation, real community seems harder to find, and difficulties with the Church have deepened into a kind of distance: many people prefer to 'do it my way', as the song put it.

Thus it is not easy to defend the importance of Church today. But if we are to get anywhere on this question, we need to tune in to the right wavelength. Most talk about Church is external or sociological: about the clergy or the bishops or the structures or the influence in society, or perhaps about outer practices and norms. All these things are real and can create problems, but none of them touches the core. That level of argument will never help us understand the Church in the light of faith. Indeed, getting stuck with that surface image of Church can even block 'faith in Christ'. The question implies, mistakenly, I think, that personal faith can do without Church; however, others identify with Church belonging and faith so much that if one gets into difficulties, the other falls as well. We need to see that the Church is the essential home and servant of faith, but that these are not one and the same thing.

I would like to suggest a few guidelines for thinking about the Church. They are attitudes that I have found necessary within myself and also when talking about this whole area with others. They are ways of escaping from the wrong wavelength.

1. **Don't judge by appearances.**
   The Church has a human dimension and is, like any person, a fragile mystery. I can never know what is really going on within a person by watching outer behaviour. I remember seeing a Muslim prostrating himself and praying in the departure lounge of an airport, and the reaction of people around was to smile with a mixture of embarrassment and superiority. But there was more than the visible. You can see someone praying. You cannot see prayer itself. And the Church is rather like that, with its rind and its core. It is human and visible and weak, but it is more than human. I can never fathom the reality of the Church from a human point of view alone.

2. **To understand it better, seek the Church at its best.**
   Nobody can deny the sinful sides of Church life, just as nobody can deny the egoism in his or her own heart. But just as we hope to be forgiven our failings and appreciated at our deepest, so we need not only compassion for dealing with the human failures of the Church, but a recognition that it exists to share Christ's gift in this world. It has the goal of liberating people to be saints. And in every generation the Church produces living mirrors of Jesus, these figures of transparent love – like 'proofs' of the true identity of the Church.

3. **Christ left his vision and his gift in human hands.**
   In the gospels Jesus deliberately chooses and forms a group of apostles, with Peter in a special position, to continue his own work. On one occasion in Matthew's Gospel (16:18), Jesus speaks of '*my* Church', and later the Risen Christ com-

plains to Saul (the future Paul) that he is 'persecuting *me*' by his attacks on the early Church (Acts 9:4). From these moments, and others in the New Testament, it is clear that Christ not only wanted to found a community with certain leaders, but that he identified himself with this community. And Matthew's Gospel ends with the promise: 'I am with you always, yes, to the end of time.' (It is worth adding that when various 'evangelical' groups claim that the written New Testament is everything and that Church does not matter, they are historically wrong: in fact the book was born from the community, not the other way round. The first generations had an oral tradition within the Church, and written texts only came later.)

4. **Don't be too shocked by the mixed field.**
This idea comes from the parable of Jesus which tells of the reaction of the farmworkers who had planted wheat only to find weeds growing together with the wheat. They want to pull up the weeds but the wise farmer says no, because 'you might pull up the wheat with it' (Matthew 13:29). Expecting perfection is an illusion. The Church is planted as a wheat field but there are also weeds. In fact Jesus expended a lot of energy persuading the apostles to face their own temptations to power and training them in a spirit of childlike service (Mark 9: 34-37). Putting all this more personally, I should not be surprised when the battles of my own heart are mirrored in some way in the human aspects of the Church. But the Church is still a wheat field, a source of wisdom and light. As Chesterton said: 'The Church has been cruel; but the world has been much more cruel', and he suggests asking 'the simple question of what the world would be like without it'.

5. **We are not asked to be Christians on our own.**
From where did any of us receive Christian faith, if not from

the Church? And, similarly, it is there that we find companionship and nourishment on the journey of faith. Indeed we human beings are more in need of others than the animals: many animals can be independent immediately after birth, but we grow slowly into language and into love only through others. Similarly, all through the New Testament there is so much about community as *the* place of finding faith and of preserving the 'memory' of Christ literally alive. Though we are all different and have varied gifts to bring, 'we are all joined to one another' in one body (Romans 12:5).

But on this topic of Church, as so often in these pages, I would end by stressing experience. Talking about 'the Church' from a distance may not help much. The Church is a community of communities, with many different kinds of expression. Find some entry point that suits you. Search out some concrete way of belonging and serving. Then *from within* you can grow into a sense of what the Church is meant to be.

12   *Why should I go to Mass? I get nothing out of it.*

For years I've had to face this question from younger people or, expressed in a different way, from their worried parents, who wonder where they have gone wrong and why their teenage children have such difficulty with 'Sunday practice'. And I've come to a few conclusions – three in particular.

1. This issue brings up a clash of approaches between generations. An older generation was brought up in a 'culture of obedience', meaning that they did what they were told by people in authority, without too much questioning. They fitted into a tradition, trusted in its wisdom, and found a lot of security there. But along comes a different generation, what we can call a 'culture of experience', and they approach all these things in a different way: if it does not make sense to me, I don't see why I should do it. This is a different way of measuring what I 'should' do. (For more in this line see Question 9.)

2. We are on the wrong track if we isolate this question about Mass from the whole context of a person's level of faith. The Second Vatican Council described the Mass as both 'summit' and 'fountain' of Christian life, meaning that it is the highest expression of faith and a nourishment for living that faith. But if a person does not already possess some 'equipment' of faith, in today's culture Mass is not going to be that summit and fountain which it can ideally be. Translating that into the language of the question, and being a bit provocative, if you bring nothing to it, don't be surprised if you get nothing out of it.

3. By its nature the Mass is a rich and complex form of worship

which has evolved over a long time in the Church, and it can seem a distant language that people may not be ready for. Centuries ago 'catechumens', or people who had not yet arrived at maturity of faith, were present only for the early parts of the Mass (the readings). The sections from the offertory onwards were reserved for committed believers. In other words, this is a 'high' and solemn prayer of the Church and it is not easy to feel part of it without some formation and some growth in faith. 'Getting nothing out of it' can well be due to a lack at this level.

Does all this mean that Mass is unimportant and that if I find it boring the obligation to attend has no meaning? Not at all. The 'obligation' is for Christian believers, in particular for those who are trying to live as Catholics. It is meant to remind them to celebrate together the Lord's new life each week – on the day of victory or Resurrection. In practice, difficulties arise when young people, who may not yet have reached a mature decision about believing in Christ, are asked to take part in something that seems so much 'beyond them'.

Should they then be allowed to opt out? Not without really reflecting on what they are doing. I like the answer I once heard from an Australian mother of teenagers. At a parents' meeting in a Catholic school, this whole thorny question came up and she surprised everyone by saying she had found the solution. It went something like this: 'I say to them that as their mother I have the right to a night's sleep. And that I can't sleep properly if they drop something that I consider essential for being a Catholic – especially if they don't find some other food for their faith. So I make a bargain with them. If they really don't want to go to Mass, I won't insist on it for a trial period *provided* they do something else to help their growth as Christians. They can join the Vincent de Paul and help with the poor. They can participate in some prayer group or bible group. It's better if they do something with others.

48

But if they insist, I'll reluctantly accept that they do something on their own, like reading a spiritual book, or practising some form of meditation. One of the girls offered to mind small children during Mass, so that their parents could attend in peace. She got through her difficulties and came back, but she still helps with the children at another Mass!'

I like that approach because it challenges people to realise that something serious is at stake, and yet it recognises that there are times when it might be counter-productive to force attendance at Mass. After all, it is meant to be the expression of what is at the heart of Christian faith, and faith is always free.

But to talk about Mass as experience is not enough. One of its difficulties is that it is such a rich set of rituals, built around the gesture of Jesus during his Last Supper: 'This is my body which will be given up for you'. During that last meal with his friends, Jesus desperately wanted to 'get through to them'. He spoke of the greatest of all loves as laying down one's life for one's friends. He also spoke of going to the Father. And his gift of himself in the bread and wine was a way of embracing the next day's Cross. And all 'for you'.

'Do this in memory of me'. What do we 'do' at Mass? We have all this eucharistic gift of Jesus, all this richness and depth – not simply the gesture, but the whole way of Christ. Not just to recall the past but to make real this total love at the heart of Christianity – or, better, at the heart of Christ. This is the core of the Mass. Yes, there is too much to appreciate.

We have come a long way from arguing about obligations or different cultures – and from 'getting nothing out of it'. Perhaps I can rephrase the challenge: if you get nothing out of Christ's gift, then start further back. Who is Jesus for you? Without a personal answer to that question, we are not ready to talk about Mass. Like the catechumens of long ago, we wait patiently until we are ready.

Finally, what might help us to be more ready? Re-reading

participation

what I wrote just now about the wealth of the Eucharist, I am struck that from the point of view of youth culture much of this is simply a foreign language. Therefore being ready means learning that language. It means basic faith in Christ, because Mass is meaningless without that. But for young people the breakthrough will come most of all through participating in some special celebrations of Mass. Unfortunately the average Sunday Mass (at least in Ireland) can be painfully unimaginative. And yet Mass can and should be a community event of prayer and power. Increasingly there are parishes that offer opportunities for special liturgies adapted to the needs of many people today, not just the young. From the special one learns to appreciate the more ordinary.

As so often, I come back to suggesting that the key answer is at the level of experience. Reading something like this can help, but finding a lived reality of faith with others makes all the difference.

13 I admit that I make mistakes but what does 'sin' mean?

Yes, there is a big difference. Put very simply, the key is God. What sin means can only be understood from within a relationship with God. 'Mistakes' seem like lonely burdens – outside that relationship. Besides, there is a tendency today to attribute wrongdoing to social or psychological factors: many criminals have had terrible times in childhood. We are right to take account of that, and to recognise the pressures on any of us that leave us unfree. But to talk about sin invites us to another level – to a liberating sense of responsibility for what we do and to a recognition of our need for healing before Christ.

There is a moment in Luke's Gospel (chapter 5) that has always helped me to understand sin. The disciples have been fishing without any success. Jesus tells them to try the other side. They pull in the greatest catch in their whole career. And faced with this full net, Peter chooses to fall at the knees of Jesus and says 'Depart from me, I am a sinful man'. Why this? Why does he not praise or thank God?

Perhaps the best moment for recognising sin is when you are in touch with the 'full net', with the wonder of life, with a sense of yourself as gift. And then sin is the shadow side, the fact that I have not lived in harmony with who I really am. The psychologist Erich Fromm has a fascinating statement: 'Destructiveness is the outcome of unlived life.' It is as if Peter, in that moment of fullness, recognised his emptiness by contrast, but more importantly, he recognised his unworthiness before Christ. The giver of the gift is present. We can change Fromm's insight: sin is an unlived relationship. It is not a question of letting myself down by some 'mistake'. It is more like letting down a friend, and so sin is something I can appreciate best when I am – like Peter – both aware of the full net and in the presence of that Friend.

It is interesting that in the New Testament the Greek word for sin is '*hamartia*', a word that comes from sport. In archery it means 'missing the mark'. What mark do we miss when we sin? Love, fullness, the hopes of Christ for us. That is the positive goal of our humanity, which our actual living can fail to reach. That falling short, when it is due to irresponsibility, is one useful image of sin.

Of course there are other ways of understanding sin: a going against our true value and call; a refusal to grow and to love; something contrary to the will of God; a preference for lonely selfishness as against the price of personhood with Christ; an uncaring attitude towards others (often rooted in fear about my own worth). In one way or another I say or live the attitude: 'to hell with everything but me!' In fact sin is very conservative, in the worst sense, because it clings to an old me and resists the newness that I am invited into by life and by the Lord.

But the real key to sin is not just psychological: it lies in the relationship to God's hopes for us. 'The glory of God is humanity fully alive' (St Irenaeus); if so, sin is the opposite, a turning away from that aliveness-in-love which, amazingly, is a cause of God's joy.

We sometimes talk about God being offended by our sin. Beware of the images lurking behind this. God does not go into bad humour or sulks. We 'offend' Christ because he has identified himself with others: 'As often as you did it to one of these you did it to me' (Matthew 25:40).

And a similar caution is needed about God's forgiveness. The human parallels can lead us astray. If I 'offend' someone and if he or she 'forgives' me, it usually means that they say 'Okay, I understand you didn't really mean it, let's start again, I won't hold it against you.' But God's forgiveness is different. There are no periods of coldness or distance. Forgiveness does not mean that God relents because I promise to improve. God has been waiting for me in love even when I was distant or cold. Forgiveness means a change in me. I let love reach and heal the zones where I was hurting myself. That love has now 'the quality of mercy' (Shakespeare) because it reaches into the self-woundedness called sin – in order to set my heart free to hope again. Forgiveness means that God's always-surprising love visits the dark areas of my life and dissolves the fear that I cannot really learn to love.

Perhaps the childhood echoes of the word 'sin' resound too long into adulthood so that we think of it mainly in terms of externals and rules. Unless we begin to recognise our sin-attitudes before the Lord, as a falling-short in a relationship and from a growth of heart, sin can seem to be just a childish notion. Instead it is central, alas, to our existence. But we are saved from that lonely 'alas' by Christ.

14 *What's the point of confession? And why to a priest?*

Think first about these various points: It helps to be really honest about myself with another person; to admit the harm I have done to others; to find support or advice in my struggles; to talk over where I am trying to grow; to find relief for my sense of guilt; to renew a relationship that has been damaged; to express my hopes for improving my life.

It also helps to be free to live more lovingly; to express sorrow for my selfishness before God and in the community; to receive Christ's healing in a concrete way; to ask for gifts I cannot give myself – forgiveness and a changed heart.

The first paragraph lists a number of 'human' reasons, which could apply to going to a counsellor or having an important conversation with a friend. The second paragraph details the more 'Christian' perspective, because the Sacrament of Reconciliation (or Confession) cannot be understood except in the light of faith in Christ.

For this most human of all the sacraments we need to keep both lists in mind. The sacrament is not merely human space for facing difficulties, but it can offer much on that level too. Today, when many people pay large sums to talk to a psychologist, it seems strange that this sacrament is on the decline everywhere – in spite of being free! Of course there is much more to confession than counselling, as is clear from that second list. But at its best this sacrament can include helpful human contact and exchange, just as in those moments when Jesus encountered people on the human level before leading them towards the deeper freedom offered by God. Think of his meeting with the tough and hurt woman at the well (John 4), where their conversation moves gradually from her initial resistance to being able to mention the brokenness of her life ('five husbands') and ends with her knowing who Jesus really is.

I see three main reasons why this sacrament seems in decline nowadays, especially for young people. The first is that they may not have had a good experience of it, as an encounter of healing and prayerfulness. The second is that many wonder why they need to confess to a priest: I will try to comment briefly on this here, but it is connected to the whole attitude to Church. (For more on this see Question 11.) The third is that there is a lot of uncertainty about what 'sin' means (already explored in Question 13).

As I remarked earlier, to understand something, it helps to consider it at its best rather than at its worst. (We all would prefer to be appreciated for our best days, not judged only on our darker moments.) Unfortunately, as regards confession, many people have bad experiences to recount. I myself 'had my nose bitten off' some years ago in a confessional in London, where I was on holidays, just because I was not dressed in clericals (and had mentioned as part of my confession that I was a priest). It was not easy to be patient but I tried to accept this attack as part of my penance!

On the more positive side, I recall many times when the sacrament has been a source of new life for me. According to the 'new' form of the sacrament, we should begin with a short passage from scripture. It means that what you have to say is secondary: first the Lord promises you love and mercy. It can also change the focus of the sacrament from embarrassing self-exposure to an echo of the many healing episodes in the gospel. Notice that nowadays the Church prefers to call this the Sacrament of Reconciliation rather than Confession. It's a significant change, which puts the emphasis on God's gift of freedom, and not on our duty of sometimes difficult honesty.

What should you say? Some short account of where you have been responsible for refusing to be faithful to Christ and caring for others. Yes, 'responsibility' is central: you were free to act differently but you did not. As children we made lists of external failures (like fighting with my brothers); as adults we can mention externals but also aim at a confession of attitudes (because I feel jealous or resentful). But what-you-say is not the key to this sacrament: what-Christ-gives is the key. Remember what was said in the previous question on 'sin' about the deeper meaning of 'forgiveness', which is not just like a human being dropping a grudge against you. It is much more like a reaching of love into the shadows of our lives.

There are two sides to this sacrament – what you bring and what the Church gives you in the name of Christ. Here's a little test. What is the most important thing you bring, or the main preparation you have to make? (And don't read ahead before pausing to think what your answer would be.)

It's *not* the confessing itself, nor preparation through self-examination. In the *Catechism of the Catholic Church* (1451) 'contrition' occupies the first place in the acts of the penitent. More crucial than what you say is your attitude of sorrow and your desire to change with God's help. This is the serious part of the sacrament for the person 'going to confession'. It might be better to call it 'going to conversion', or 'going to Christ's healing'. When you come to this sacrament, sin – what you have done or not done – is already a story of the past. The new story is the meeting between your hopes and Christ's healing. Reconciliation needs two sides.

But why to a priest?

Because Christian faith starts from the human Jesus, so all sacraments echo the Incarnation. Because he wanted his healing work to continue through his community, the Church, Jesus said to his disciples after the Resurrection: 'Receive the Holy Spirit – whose sins you shall forgive, they are forgiven' (John 20:22-23). Because we have offended others and damaged the community which is represented by the priest. Because we are helped more through an honest conversation with the priest, who in this special moment stands for Christ, than through private confession to God (which is fine in itself, and indeed there are different moments of 'confession' in every Mass, at the beginning and just before Communion).

But I come back to the need to experience this sacrament in a mature way in order to appreciate its depth. Many young people have found this possible on special occasions – pilgrimages, retreats, before marriage, and so on. It is the most personal of the encounters with Christ which we call sacraments. Don't be afraid to ask a priest to give you some time, even outside the traditional confession box, so that this gift can truly meet your hopes.

15 Why should we not have sex before marriage if we care for each other?

Let's start from the wider world around us now. Everyone agrees that there are powerful sexual pressures on people today, through the media, advertising, and the mobility of life-styles. I think there is also something deeper at work. If there was less pre-marital sex a generation or two ago, it was not simply because those pressures were not so strong. It was not only because a more traditional society was supportive of fidelity. Without going into all the details of so-called 'post-modernity', I am convinced that we are living with a very different cultural mood than we were a generation ago. (See Question 9 on generation differences.) Part of this moment is a new distrust of anything larger than the self. 'My' autonomy becomes central. And from this new isolation 'an ideology of intimacy' is born. This whole dimension of life seems to become the only hope for me.

If this is true, we cannot find a good answer about sexuality today unless we notice some of the assumptions that we breathe in, like air, from the culture around us. And I'm trying to say that it's deeper than just the 'bad influence' from the media. Sexuality has become a way of overcoming a deeper loneliness, more acute today than even thirty years ago. According to the English sociologist Anthony Giddens, there has been a 'transformation of intimacy' when human trust is no longer nourished by a network of community, and so the 'opening out of the individual to the other' becomes a key way of searching for identity today. Where old forms of social belonging collapse, one result is a huge and excessive concentration on sexuality. So, in tackling the difficult issue of sexual morality, I admit that some of what I am going to say will seem incredible and unliveable to many honest and good friends of mine. In a sense, I *am* living in a different world.

I want to respond to the question on two levels – the human and the Christian. In other words, first I want to say why pre-marital sex seems mistaken – even outside the light of faith. I admit that it's difficult to convince people of these more human arguments: in practice it is much clearer when you approach the question from inside a commitment to Christ. However, there are important points to be made simply in terms of human experience.

At its simplest sex can be too easy and therefore deceptive. If treated casually, it forgets two important areas: permanence and tenderness. The whole area of man-woman relationships is going to be central in most people's lives, as *the* learning space for love, for going beyond our ingrained egoisms, and finding a long road of healing. So it is a very precious area of our humanity, and it is wrong to treat it lightly. Sexual relations, outside the permanent commitment of marriage, can of course be deep and powerful; but by choosing that road – without even realising it – you can be learning to treat (long-term) fidelity and permanence as secondary to (short-term) self-fulfilment.

The Guardian newspaper (regarded as a very liberal influence) has commented on contemporary trends: 'Outside a loving relationship sex is in reality deeply unsatisfying [especially since it] has become our sad, misguided substitute for intimacy.' And, I would add, for tenderness. Tenderness means a whole range of human intimacy that does not necessarily involve strong sexual expression. It expresses care, affection and love. It can be a matter of words, or silence, or gentle physical closeness. I have heard from many young people that they (sometimes secretly) prefer tenderness to sex. They realise that they need to grow there first. And the danger is that jumping to the top rung of the ladder, so to speak, means that you don't learn this important middle range of relationship. Indeed I have known marriages to be in trouble because these middle rungs of honesty and mutual knowing were neglected.

Coming to the Christian perspective there is no doubt that

the whole tradition values sexuality deeply and because of that sees it as a treasure to be guarded for the God-blessed union of marriage. There is no doubt about the message of the Bible against irresponsible sexual activity: from the human heart 'evil intentions come' which lead to immorality (Mark 7: 22); 'nobody who indulges in promiscuity can inherit anything of the Kingdom of God' (Ephesians 5:5). But it is more than simply a matter of obedience to an important norm. A Christian is someone who knows something of the attitudes and heart of Christ. I have never known a young person who had arrived at some kind of mature faith and who did not *intuitively* realise that sex outside marriage is out of tune with being a follower of Christ. You can understand something within yourself without being able to explain it successfully. At its deepest, when you look at Jesus on the Cross you know – beyond mere argument – that all real love involves a letting go, a note of sacrifice. (See Question 12 on Mass.)

Many years ago (it must have been about 1980), I was present when Jean Vanier gave a retreat for university students. Jean, a Canadian, has spent his life creating communities, called l'Arche, for the handicapped and speaks with the authority of his deep dedication. A student asked him about pre-marital sex, and his indirect way of answering has stayed with me ever since. It went more or less like this. If you have any major decision to make and you want it to be in harmony with Christian faith, then there are three questions to ask yourself.

1. Is what I am proposing to do really in tune with my best and deepest self? If there are any doubts, pause and listen, otherwise you are not being honest with your own heart and conscience.
2. Is what I am choosing in harmony with what I know of Jesus Christ? To answer this put yourself in prayer before him and ask for light.

3. The decision I make will steer my life in a certain direction. What I choose now will have a long-term impact on me. Let me ask myself what the result will be on my compassion for the weak and wounded of this world, the poor and rejected. Is my decision going to leave me more open or more hard and closed towards them?

Great food for mature thought there!

To end on a lighter note, here are three bits of wisdom from G. K. Chesterton. He remarked once that anyone knocking on a prostitute's door is actually looking for God!

Again, he commented that 'the moment sex ceases to be a servant it becomes a tyrant': it is a magnificent language of permanent love, but it can easily become a dictatorial toy.

And on the impossible hope of treating this whole area with cool detachment he says that someone 'who asks us to have no emotion in sex is asking us to have no emotion in emotion . . . he does not know what he is talking about'.

16 *Why should I pray, and how?*

W hy?
- Because without some contact with God life easily becomes empty and loveless.
- Because Jesus himself did.
- Because there is a huge hunger in you waiting to find food.
- Because often we are scattered and astray and we need an anchor, a Presence to heal us and lift us up.
- Because if faith is true, and if the Spirit lives within us, and if we are here to learn to love like Christ, then prayer is where we remember who we are, who God is, what it is all about.
- Because if you are invited to friendship with Christ, why hold back? 'I call you friends because I have made known everything to you' (John 15:15). Perhaps spiritual life really begins when you realise that this invitation is addressed to you, and that your friendship with Christ needs nourishment through contact like any friendship.

How?
- By saying the great prayers like the Our Father or the Hail Mary slowly, with your whole self.
- By asking (in those prayers) for the big things you need, strength to keep loving, courage to forgive, and so on.
- By going beyond 'saying prayers' (which are fine, but can get you into a rut and block you from a deeper relationship).
- By finding your own way of being quiet and attentive with the Lord.
- Or, to take a gospel example, by learning to be less like the anxious and bothered Martha and more like her sister Mary, who just 'sat at the feet of Jesus and listened to his words' (Luke 10:39).

To put it strongly, adult praying means getting beyond both babble and bargaining – the tendency to 'use many words'(criticised by Jesus himself) and the image of the prayer relationship as negotiation for favours. Again the gospel is so realistic on this: 'Your Father knows what you need before you ask' (Matthew 6:8). Prayer, as it becomes more personal, changes you – it transforms your heart and your horizon.

Yes, but how can we do this in practice? All this is ideal but it doesn't really tell us what we can do to pray.

I suggest two starting points that go well together: *stillness* and *scripture*. By stillness I mean various ways of gathering the self into being more present and more ready to listen to the word of God. You have to be patient with yourself and use an anchor to create inner silence. Whatever 'anchor' you choose, don't rush it: give it several minutes at least. Otherwise you won't reach the level of quiet that makes 'remaining' in prayer so much easier.

What do I mean by an anchor? I offer three kinds: visual, physical, verbal. For instance, you could just watch the flickering of a candle; or, with your eyes closed, pay attention to the coming and going of your breath, the bodily movement in and out. It is a very basic way of 'anchoring' your attention, in a spirit not of stern will-power but of gentle awareness. Or you could choose a line from Scripture and repeat it again and again, like a recurring rhythm of sounds within you. For instance: 'I call you by your name: you are mine' (Isaiah 43), or 'The Lord is my light and my help; whom shall I fear?' (Psalm 26), or 'Like a deer longing for running streams, my soul thirsts for you, my God' (Psalm 42). The secret is to pick *one* simple focus and let it lead you slowly into stillness. These lines from Scripture, echoing for several minutes within you, might surprise you with the depth of the sense of intimacy, or trust, or desire that they engender.

The other great breakthrough into personal prayer comes when you learn to 'pray the Scriptures', particularly the gospels. Each meeting with Jesus there can invite *you* to imagine yourself in that encounter or episode, to be present, to be yourself there, to speak to Jesus and to listen to him.

One famous example is the visit of Jesus to the house of Zacchaeus (Luke 19). Although Zacchaeus wanted to see Jesus he was blocked by his smallness (we can all identify with that), but he made a special effort (like your effort to read even these lines): he climbed a tree. Jesus saw him there, told him to 'hurry' down and let him stay at his house. Zacchaeus, the gospel tells us, did this 'with joy'. Already the surprise of being recognised and needed had changed him.

How can you make this personal? In whatever way attracts you. I remember a young man called David taking this scene in prayer and discovering surprising sides to it. David found himself bringing Jesus into his house in a special sense: there were all sorts of doors with labels on them: loneliness, family, sexuality, friendships, hopes, dark memories, and so on. In this fantasy meditation he was about to give Jesus a tour of these rooms, some of them locked, when Jesus said: 'Let me show you round your own house, telling you how *I* see all these areas of your life – because I know them all already!' And that was the beginning of a quietly amazing prayer of accepting himself as deeply understood and loved by the Lord.

Prayer can mean more than you think: but it needs a little courage and time to enter this experience. Not everyone has David's imagination. But try it out for yourself in your own way. Or, as the gospel says, 'Come and see'.

PART III

UNDERSTANDING FAITH

Some Theological Questions

17 *Are all religions the same?*

There are, of course, deep areas shared by all religions. A sense of God as good and of humanity in need of help is at the heart of every great religious tradition. Perhaps centuries ago missionaries went out with the idea that Hinduism or Islam were simply the work of the devil: no Catholic listening to Pope John Paul on his numerous foreign journeys and seeing him meeting leaders of others religions could hold that view any more! Nowadays the Catholic Church has come to recognise the presence of genuine religious wisdom in the non-Christian traditions, and that the Spirit of God is at work in every human being, bringing forth freedom and love.

In recent years, my own work has allowed me to travel more than I ever imagined when I was a child, even if not as much as the Pope! But I have managed to visit countries where Christianity was very different from anything I knew (like the Orthodox Church in Ethiopia), or where it was practised by a small minority (like India or, more so, Iran). What these personal memories add up to is that the world religions seem much less alike when you get to see them close up.

Let me offer you three quick pictures. In India I sometimes visited Hindu temples and was always struck by the many activities going on: they were crowded places with statues everywhere, of goddesses with many arms, for instance, and with busy worshippers, chanting, offering incense, candles, flowers and so on. To me it seemed like having a different face of God for every season – the sense of the divine seemed very varied and very human.

In contrast to this, I remember standing in what is called the most beautiful mosque in the world, at Esfahan in Iran, and being overwhelmed by the magnificence of that silent and empty space. The walls were covered with intricate designs in brilliant colours, but no representation, no images. Worshippers came quietly and prostrated themselves several times. So different from the Hindu temple, because the Islamic sense of God is of distance, reverence, awe, the Holy One who asks for prayer and obedient living.

My third memory is of a Catholic church in India, a fairly old-fashioned church with statues of saints and a life-sized realistic crucifix. I was there one day when a group of children came on a school outing with their teacher. They included both Hindus and Muslims. The Muslims were amazed by all the statues, but the Hindu children were only surprised, and even frightened, by the figure on the cross. They asked the teacher what it represented, and she replied that she thought it was Jesus Christ. She looked at me for help and I found myself explaining in a few words the story of the crucifixion and resurrection, and that Christians believe Jesus to be the Son of God. Put yourself in my shoes before such a group of children, and you may realise how difficult it was to be understood.

And I saw then how different Christianity is, in spite of all the deep things that we share with other religions. You could explain some of the differences between religions in terms of different cultures, just as an African Mass is often much longer and more lively than the same Mass in Ireland. But before the crucifix, there was a more fundamental difference: no other religion says that God loved us so much that he became one of us, and then died for us. This is radically different. It makes a huge claim. It is rooted in history, not in some founder's experience or inspiration. The other religions are profound expressions of human hunger, and even of encounter with the Spirit of God. But they stay on the level of a wisdom that hopes and searches for God. Christianity is about God coming to search for us, in the only language that really reaches our hearts – the language of a person in love.

There is much more to say…. This is a bit short and simple. I have not mentioned the Jewish tradition from which we come in Christ. But the key difference of Christian faith lies in that One Person, and in the meaning of that crucifixion.

18 If we know about evolution, how can we believe that God created the world the way the Bible decribes?

There is only a seeming conflict between the biblical picture and the theory of evolution, but it is an interesting example of where we need to outgrow superficial approaches and black-and-white interpretations. Science and the Bible offer different approaches to reality. The Bible is not attempting to give a physical history of the universe, but is trying to communicate the deep meaning of existence as a gift of God: the Book of Genesis does this by telling a story that does not have to be taken literally in all its details. Science, in contrast, offers descriptions rather than meanings, precise data and conclusions rather than a philosophical narrative.

A quick story might give flesh to this point. I remember that my father was in hospital once with heart problems. The specialist showed me the results of an electrocardiogram, with all its graphs and jagged lines, and described to me the kind of man my father was – with these tensions and pressures, and so on. What he was saying was true, but it was hardly a full picture of my father! Science offers that kind of knowledge of humanity and our universe. But what the Bible talks about is God's relationship to us all and to our world: it is more like my personal knowledge of my father than the accurate but limited knowledge of the heart specialist. So we are dealing with two different aspects or interpretations, two kinds of truth.

Another story comes to mind. St Joan of Arc was tried (and indeed burnt at the stake) for being a witch: her theological and political judges did not believe that her 'voices' came from God. There was a moment in her trial when the prosecutor thought he had pinned her down. He put it to her (as lawyers always say) that her voices came from her imagination, and Joan replied, 'Perhaps yes'. 'Ah', said the delighted prosecutor, 'so you admit it: the voices don't come from God at all.' But Joan replied brilliantly, 'And could the good God who gave me imagination, not also use it?'

The parallel is simple: could God in creating the universe not also 'use' evolution?

In the Book of Genesis, there are two stories of creation in the early chapters, and they do not agree in every respect. For instance in one account Adam and Eve are created simultaneously, but in the other Adam comes first and then there is the famous rib! But this variety shows that the authors were trying out different ways of interpreting our existence, and they certainly were not claiming to offer eye-witness accounts of what happened millions or thousands of years before. The aim is not historical or biological exactitude but theological meaning: life as good and as coming from God.

It helps also if we realise that these creation stories were shaped at a particular moment of Jewish history, almost certainly during the Exile in Babylon. It was a time of national disaster, when the pagan religion of Babylon was able to gloat over the defeated god of the Jews. And this religion had an elaborate myth about the origin of the world: they saw it as coming from a war between Marduk, a god of light, and some sinister dragon – from the blood of the dragon Marduk made human beings. The Genesis account was formed to answer this, and above all to insist, even in a moment of tragedy, on the people's faith in God's continuing presence in creation: everything exists, especially humanity, so that love can flow. In opposition to the pagan picture of gods in struggle, Genesis pictures God creating in serene power and freedom, offering a relationship to Adam and Eve (which they resisted and damaged, but that is another story) and, above all, delighted with creation: 'God saw all that was made, and indeed it was very good' (Genesis 1:31).

To know something of this background will help us to understand that the Creation story is not trying to be true in its details but rather in its deep vision of God and the world.

But there is another issue here that needs clarifying. By 'creation' we do not mean just the beginning of our world and our reality, but their continuing existence now. To reduce 'creation' to some long-ago beginning event is to miss the point! The question was about the picture of creation in the Bible, and this means much more than the Book of Genesis. Other parts of the Old Testament talk about creation in the sense of God's slow shaping of people, their liberation from evil and for love. Thus creation is not a once-off event, but like a work of art that continues in each moment.

The Australian physicist Paul Davies received a major prize in 1995 for his books on science and religion, and in his acceptance speech touched on some misunderstandings of creation. Many people, he said, 'imagine a Superbeing who deliberates for all eternity, then presses a metaphysical button and produces a huge explosion. I believe this image is entirely misconceived.... If there is a meaning or purpose to existence, as I believe there is, we are wrong to dwell too much on the originating event. The big bang is sometimes referred to as "the creation", but in truth nature has never *ceased* to be creative.'

So, far from being the denial of creation, evolution (if it is true, and this is still far from certain) would be one way of understanding how creation still continues today. Before leaving this whole topic, it is important to mention that we are also responsible for creation. As human beings, the summit of creation according to the biblical vision, we are invited into a kind of co-creation with God. The planet is in our hands. In recent years we have come to a much greater understanding of the earth's vulnerability and of how susceptible it is to damage. Indeed, even our own personal lives are a kind of co-creation, cooperating with God's grace in shaping our own selves. In the words of St Paul,

'We are God's work of art, created in Christ Jesus to live the good life as from the beginning he has meant us to live it' (Ephesians 2:10).

Yes, we have come a long way from surface arguments about evolution, and that is right. As with many other topics of faith, we understand much better when we go deeper and find the riches behind the outer rind.

19 Science can explain everything. Why should we still believe in God?

I want to put two stories side by side, one famous and the other a memory of my own. Nearly two centuries ago, when the Marquis de Laplace presented his study of structure in the universe to Napoleon, the Emperor remarked that God seemed to be omitted from his system. Laplace's celebrated reply was, 'Sir, I had no need for that hypothesis'. It sums up a whole attitude that is still very widespread: that everything can be explained by scientific observation, and that there is no need for any other kind of questioning.

Against this I remember an occasion years ago when I was studying philosophy. We had a wise old professor called Thomas Gornall, an expert in the Thomist tradition of thinking about God. However there was one student who had just finished a degree in science and was perhaps a little full of himself. One day he came out with a long and impressive account of evolution as offering a whole other approach to reality. Fr Gornall listened patiently, before replying with a touch of irony: 'Perhaps you haven't really started philosophising yet. We are asking another question. You are *describing* one process. We are trying to *explain* the very existence of reality, of everything. You have to move from "how" to "why", and this big "why" is beyond science.'

Putting the two incidents side by side, the key message is not to confuse different approaches and different levels of inquiry – music is more than vibrations in the air, poetry is more than marks on paper, and love is more than biological reactions.

Certainly there were a few centuries of tension between religion and science, starting from the time of Galileo. He was misunderstood and even badly treated by the Church because at that time people could not grasp the simple point Fr Gornall was

; in Question 13 I have tried to show how
 risky and how we should not have an image
 going into a sulk and then deciding to 'make

hese possible misunderstandings, what do we
 from? I think the basic answer is fairly easy.
 world and see the many forms of evil, suffering,
 ce and oppression, or what the novelist Saul
 'disappointed life'. In spite of much goodness,
 very wrong. Listen also to your own heart. There
 g is wrong. As St Paul so honestly put it, 'I cannot
 my own behaviour. I fail to carry out the things I
 ... [because] sin lives in me.... Who will rescue me?
 be to God through Jesus Christ our Lord!' (Romans
 24). To understand salvation you have to get in touch
 e two zones of failure: the scandals of our human histo-
 e more personal slide into egoism.
 ed those two faces of evil are linked: most of the large-
 uffering in the world comes from human choices of one
 r another. For instance, even the dehumanising division of
 lanet into rich and poor worlds is not inevitable: it could be
 rent *if* we had the will to change our ways.
 Yes, we have a responsibility for our own lives and for our
 rld. But salvation is something greater than our decisions. It
 arts from God's gift rather than from our effort. It means a heal-
 g of our hearts by God. I am convinced that the best way to
 understand salvation is to think of all those many moments in
the gospels when Jesus heals people. We are all paralysed or blind
or deaf in various ways, and salvation means that the love of God,
so transparent in Jesus, reaches us and heals us. Through Jesus we
are restored to what God intended us to be: free for love. But we
are slow learners and it is a long journey to embrace that gift
called salvation.

Finally, why the Cross? Why did Jesus save us by that kind of

making. Before Galileo's time science thought of itself as looking
for purpose in the universe. Then its approach shifted to verifying external data, and to being more interested in cause and effect
than in some ultimate purpose. The very success of this 'empirical' method created the impression that there was no other road
to truth. Taking an accurate look at reality was everything.

Thus science developed enormously but in a limited field:
describing and even explaining particular aspects of the universe.
However, that approach – Laplace was right – felt no need to ask
bigger questions. As Hamlet says to his less imaginative friend,
'there are more things in heaven and earth, Horatio, than are
dreamt of in your philosophy'. We come back to the central point
about not confusing methods, and of remaining open to horizons
not dreamt of in empirical science.

The road to scientific truth, if it stays on the level of observation, will not bring us to religious truth. They are different wavelengths of our humanity. Indeed, scientists have found that there
are two hemispheres in our brain that work along different lines:
the left brain specialises in clear and logical analysis but the right
side is more intuitive and musical. Perhaps the very success of
empirical science has caused us to equate truth with the 'left'
approach only and to distrust that 'right' wavelength of our
thinking.

In the last few decades huge changes have taken place within
science and its relations with religion. The old method of Galileo
and Newton is no longer central, at least for the frontiers of
physics or astronomy. A more recent scientific method deals with
what is beyond mere observation. What is called 'positivism' has
gone into decline, meaning the approach that reduced all reality
to surface visibility. I don't understand all the implications of 'relativity' or 'quantum mechanics' but I learn from scientists that
the old separation between empirical and philosophical questions
is out of date (Fr Gornall would be excited!). Science itself has
become much more open to mystery.

Science, old and new, assumes that the world is somehow intelligible. Or, as Einstein himself remarked, 'the eternal mystery of the world is its comprehensibility'. But science today is much more aware of the limited nature of its hypotheses and, faced with the complexity of the cosmos, of how little is really certain. In such a situation (I borrow here from the physicist Polkinghorne) 'the ability of understanding to outrun explanation' is true both of advanced science and of religious faith.

Of course problems still arise today, mainly in relation to the application of technology (genetic engineering or ecology, for instance). In fact, because of these ethical problems a new mutual respect is developing between the Church and the world of science. The tone of this new dialogue is captured in the words of Pope John Paul II:

> Religion is not founded on science nor is science an extension of religion. Each should possess its own principles.... Science can purify religion from error and superstition; religion can purify science from idolatry and false absolutes. Each can draw the other into a wider world, a world in which both can flourish. (from a letter to Fr George Coyne)

So, that initial question seems out of date when we see the new horizons emerging today.

20

Years ago I saw a
strip' style, prod
Christian group. But it
of the images that can ha
angry God, with a big stick
the stealing of the apple in t
a whole long line of children a
something wrong and nobody h
ward and says he will take the pun
ones. And the next picture was the
God looking on from on high.

How distorted can our imaginatio
you can find occasional metaphors that p
'satisfaction', but the simplest statement is
the world so much that he gave his onl
Whatever our understanding of salvation, it h
with the two roots – love and gift – as that con
did not. The death of Jesus is not the 'satisfacti
God who wants a painful sacrifice.

Perhaps we need to clear the ground before stati
what salvation means. We must rid ourselves not only o
picture of God, but of other legalistic or commercial im
can block a richer sense of salvation. The word 'redempti
instance, echoes the old custom of ransoming slaves or pris
by paying a price for them; and yes, we are ransomed in a se
by Christ, but we must not take the parallel too literally. Indee
much of our talk about God uses images from human situations
that are both helpful and unhelpful. Take 'reconciliation', anoth-

death? There is no logical answer or, to put it better, only within the logic of God's love can we begin to understand. Even the question is a bit misleading: we are not saved by the Cross in the sense of mere suffering; rather, we are saved by the love with which Jesus embraced the Cross and 'died for us' (Romans 5:8). And it is important to add that we are saved by the Cross *and* Resurrection of Jesus, in other words by his victory over evil and entry into new life for us. Salvation means sharing that journey of Jesus. On our own we were powerless to escape from the vicious circle of our egoism, but Christ restores us, so to speak, to our true selves before God. If healing is one side of salvation, liberation for life and love is another. Being saved by Christ is not just a cosy sense of being all right, but an urgent entry into new life. And there is one way of measuring our response to salvation in practice: 'we know that we have passed out of death and into life because we love' (1 John 3:14).

On this whole question, even more than usual, I am aware of how sketchy my answer has been. It is an enormous field. So, before leaving it, I want to borrow from the theologian Sebastian Moore who has written several books on salvation. He tells of a preacher who pointed to the crucifix and exclaimed 'What a way to run a universe!' The surprise of this remark led him to realise how different the wisdom of God is. There is no question of placating God through the death of Jesus but rather of setting us free from our fear of death and our more unspoken fear of a loveless life. Moore goes further, and suggests that if I put myself prayerfully before the crucifix I can discover two deep truths: I see that I crucify life in me through my refusal to love, and I see in Jesus the person I do not dare to be. In the crucifix I see a double image – a mirror of human self-destruction and of God's love liberating us all from this darkness.

This is not something to be thought about in a surface way but something to be pondered quietly. And then comes the crown of salvation – the Resurrection. As the medieval writer Meister

Eckhart put it: 'God enjoys himself and wants us to join him'. And St Irenaeus said the same thing in different words: 'God's glory is humanity fully alive'. Salvation, then, means the gift of God, allowing us to move beyond our self-made prisons into the fullness for which we are intended, both here and hereafter.

A salvation that remains closed within this world does not make sense. But that is another topic. (See Questions 24 and 25 on resurrection and after-life.)

21

'It is no good giving reasons for believing in God if that God is a monster who condemns people to hell for ever.'

This is a real sentence from a real letter of a young person deeply worried about hell. It needs to be said again and again that God only created what was 'very good' (Genesis 1:31), and *therefore* God did not create hell. Whatever hell means it is a human creation! It is born from our capacity to say a total 'no' to love. It is a horrible outcome of *our* freedom, not a divine choice. We can say that God never condemns anyone to hell against their will: they opt for it themselves and condemn themselves.

Around this terrifying possibility of an eternal 'no' has arisen a whole host of images and pictures. And much of this imagery about fire and devils can be superficial and unhelpful. Especially if it awakens unhealthy worry and fear in the childish part of our imagination. The adult approach is to see that our life involves a dramatic choice, between giving and grabbing, between self as the centre, or learning to trust and to care. But more important still is keeping our eyes on Jesus and realising that this is our only reliable image of God for Christians. 'We love because he first loved us' (1 John 4:19): that sentence says it all.

'Can everyone be saved?' the same letter asked. There is a sentence in St Paul's first letter to Timothy: 'God wants all to be saved.' So it is perfectly in tune with Catholic faith to hope that this is really true, that salvation can in some way include everyone, even the worst criminals of history, like Hitler. Somehow God's love may win and hearts be changed, and open to love for ever, which is the meaning of heaven.

In *Crossing the Threshold of Hope* the Pope tackles this question head on and says something very strong and consoling: 'Even when Jesus says of Judas the traitor that it would be better if he had not been born (Matthew 26:24), this does not have to mean that Judas is eternally damned.' And the Pope adds that the official Church has always been silent on the question of anyone actually being in hell. (So in this respect we can forget about some of the more imaginative saints and their visions: they are simply *not* the sources of Revelation.)

Hell is certainly mentioned in Scripture, even by Jesus. Is this simply an extreme way of waking us up to the choices we have to make in this life? Like a loving parent exaggerating the danger in order to warn a child about the perils of crossing the road without looking: it might be the only way to make the danger real.

We are perfectly entitled to believe and hope that hell may be 'empty' and will remain 'uninhabited' for ever. But even saying that implies that it is a 'place' with all sorts of features like fire. Hell (as a possibility) is a state of human hatred that insists on staying frozen and unmelted by God's love. It's as if God gives us this dangerous freedom to reject love, to opt for hatred for ever. Perhaps nobody ever really does this for ever, in spite of all the horrible things people do. Perhaps God's love can, in some way, eventually melt even the toughest 'no'. Or is God somehow powerless before this gift of human freedom taken to its utmost evil? We don't know. We can hope that hell will never be an eternal reality for anyone. But if hell (as a possibility) is taken seriously, it means this human rejection of love pushed to its full conclusion. As I said earlier, God never 'sends' anyone to hell against that person's will. So forget all those lurking images about a judge being in bad form and giving a severe sentence. Hell is a prison chosen by the prisoners there, something that represents a defeat for God's 'will to save all'. But because God respects our freedom to close the heart totally, the doors of hell are locked, so to speak, on the inside.

22 Can we trust that the gospels tell the true story of Jesus?

Pause first on the simple truth that we have more than one gospel. The variety of the four texts is clear evidence that they were not composed simply to record facts or to provide a biography of Jesus. If that were the case one would have been enough. Instead they offer selected memories about Jesus – preserved within the community who believed him to be the Risen Lord.

So, nobody would claim that the gospels are like reporters' transcripts of the preaching of Jesus. The four accounts were written down only *after* being part of the oral tradition of preaching by the first generation of Christians. Therefore they are the memory of the community, and its way of passing on its vision. The fact that they are expressions of faith means that episodes are recounted with a certain purpose – to communicate the good news about Jesus.

Besides, the stories the evangelists remembered about Jesus were put together, in the early Church, to serve various communities. This is the reason for the fascinating differences between the different gospels. Matthew's Gospel, for instance, is much more Jewish in its references and approach – because of his audience – and he portrays Jesus mainly as a teacher. Luke's Gospel, however, was for the non-Hebrew Gentiles, and so it stresses the joy of salvation reaching out to all people. Most experts think that Mark's Gospel was written to help the 'catechumens' of Rome, those who were thinking of converting to the Christian faith, in spite of all the persecutions. The key to this gospel is the full identity of Jesus: at first he appears to be a healer; then in the mathematical centre of the gospel (chapter 8) he is recognised as the Messiah, and again, at the end, the Roman centurion recognises even the shocking figure on the Cross as 'in truth a Son of God' (15:39).

Scholars who have studied the question of what is historically basic in the gospels all agree that some words and some moments are interpretations in the light of faith, rather than factually accurate accounts. But this should not be disturbing – unless somebody has a very 'fundamentalist' or literal approach to Scripture. Don't we all tell true stories in slightly different ways for different audiences? But the reality is the same. In a similar way the four gospels offer a rich variety of interpretations of the life of Jesus, but they repeat many of the same events that mark his life and death.

The few non-scriptural references to Jesus mention that he was put to death. But we have to depend on the gospels for practically all our knowledge of him. In spite of the fact that they do not try to offer modern-style accuracy, the historical picture of Jesus emerging from these pages is very credible, and this is now the judgement even of non-believing experts working in the field of Scripture.

23 What picture of Jesus emerges from the gospel stories?

In earlier generations a lot of work was done on Scripture to separate the bare bones of history from the possible interpretations of faith in the gospels. It was an impossible task and has become unfashionable among experts.

However, a short answer to this question can outline the basic facts about Jesus that even a non-believing historian would seldom dispute.

The name Jesus means 'one who saves'. When he was about thirty he began to preach and gather followers. Until then he had been a carpenter. He was a layman in the sense of not belonging to one of the priestly groups within the Jewish religion; this was a source of tension when he gained a special reputation as preacher and healer. His everyday, spoken language would have been Aramaic, but he seems to have been able to read the Hebrew of the Old Testament. (The Gospels were written down in Greek, because of the later expansion of Christian faith into the wider world of Greek culture.)

Several of the first followers of Jesus had previously been disciples of John the Baptist, and Jesus came to be baptised by John in the River Jordan. John had preached an austere message of repentance for the nation and this baptism was a ceremony of accepting the need for conversion because the judgement of God was coming quickly. In the period of his earliest preaching Jesus also practised a form of baptism but seems not to have continued with this throughout the two or three years of his ministry. In place of the strong emphasis on fear in the preaching of John, Jesus put a new note of joy and trust in God. But he continued John's message of a call to conversion for the whole people and not just for individuals.

What did he speak of in his preaching and how? He spoke frequently of the 'Kingdom' and he nearly always used 'parables' when speaking to large numbers of people. The kingdom pointed to a new relationship with God, where God would 'reign' in people's lives, changing their hearts gradually, leading them into a new relationship with others as well. God emerged from the parables as intimate and merciful, seeking out those who were wounded or lost or sinful. The parables were a typical way of communicating in that culture, using puzzling stories to wake people into a realisation of religious realities. They nearly always included an element of surprise and unexpectedness.

As a teacher the message of Jesus was both inviting and challenging. It spoke of God in very familiar terms, even as 'Abba' (an Aramaic equivalent of Daddy). It stressed God's tenderness and unconditional love for all. But Jesus also made demands, especially on those who wanted to embrace his way of life more deeply: they were to lose themselves, to become trusting like children, to set aside the urge to be powerful. They were to go beyond a merely legal observance of religion and live a new and demanding quality of heart. If God loved them and forgave them, then they were to love others, even their enemies, and forgive them. The unity of these two loves was at the core of the new life that Jesus spoke of so often.

But Jesus did more than speak. His actions, as we say, spoke louder than words. He broke many of the customs of his society and shocked the rigid religious leaders. Reading the gospels we do not always recognise the little details that would have been such a surprise. For instance, touching a leper was taboo and put one into the category of the ritually unclean (Mark 1:41). Or, against the strict prohibition against even picking fruit to eat on the sabbath, Jesus announced a priority of human need over legalism: the sabbath is intended to serve us, not the other way around (Mark 2:27). Jesus also became notorious for the company he kept! As one scholar in the field, John Meier, has put it, Jesus 'delighted in eating with the religious low-life of his day' (I should acknowledge that I am indebted to Professor Meier for much in this whole answer).

Among the actions of Jesus miracles had a special place, not just as acts of kindness in healing people but as a 'sign' (the word is used especially in John's Gospel) of the presence of the Kingdom – meaning a new closeness of God – and of the new levels of love which are possible for all people.

On the more spiritual level Jesus was transparently a man of prayer, sometimes spending nights in solitude on the mountain, and rooted in a special sense of his 'Father'. Since this particular answer is attempting to remain within the 'historically' accepted facts about Jesus, it does not enter the deeper realm of the meaning of that relationship with the Father, or examine the way in which Jesus understood his own identity as 'Son'.

As time went on the followers of Jesus increased in number. There was an inner circle of twelve called into special roles as 'apostles'. But there were many others, including women, who travelled with him on his journeys. Jesus himself was never married but in the context of the culture of the time, his 'easy approach to women' (Meier) was very different from the usual style of a religious teacher.

How did people view him? Within the biblical tradition he was often seen as a 'prophet', which does not mean someone who sees into the future, but someone with a powerful spiritual message for the present. Many of the major prophets had been reformers, recalling the people to the revelation of God and its implications for just living. Some of the prophets had been put to death for causing trouble – as Jesus would be.

Which brings us to his trial and crucifixion. It is on this point that the four gospels have most unity and they also give most space to describing the last days of Jesus. There is no need to summarise such a familiar story here. Instead we can end this answer with a few comments on significant historical aspects of the Passion. There was some kind of nocturnal or early morning sitting of the religious court at the Temple, where Jesus was accused of various forms of blasphemy and disobedience to the law of God. Then he was brought before Pontius Pilate, who was prefect of Judaea for the ten years between 26 and 36 AD. Because this Roman official had no interest in the internal religious affairs of the people he ruled, the charge against Jesus had to be changed into a political one: Jesus was framed as some kind of Jewish rebel who claimed to be a king. Pilate did not at first cooperate with the desires of the Temple authorities for a death sentence (which they had lost the power to impose) but eventually gave way. Jesus was first scourged, which was seen as a cruel form of mercy, because it would hasten the process of dying. The method of crucifixion was sometimes to tie people to the cross where they could linger for days. Nailing Jesus to the wood meant a shorter agony. Since the next day was a special feast for the Jews, to leave corpses hanging overnight was unacceptable. But, as the gospel recounts, when the soldiers came to break the legs of those crucified with him, thus causing a collapse of the body and suffocation, they found Jesus already dead.

The Resurrection lies beyond the scope of this answer. It is dealt with in the next question.

24 If the Resurrection of Jesus is so important, can we be sure of it?

Yes, the Resurrection is the hinge of Christian faith. As we will also see in the next question, everything hangs on this *event*. And yet it was an event without direct witnesses. You may occasionally see paintings of Jesus rising, like an explosion of light, from the tomb, with soldiers falling to the ground. But the gospels never describe that moment. Instead they tell of the Risen Jesus coming to his friends, and what it means is stranger and deeper than those pictures of the moment of Resurrection.

There are ancient tales of various gods dying and rising but it was never claimed that they were historically true. Christian faith stands or falls on the Resurrection being true in some real and concrete way. It cannot be just the Spirit-filled imagination of the disciples. Some sceptics argued that the apostles did not want to go back to fishing and therefore invented a good story! The obvious reply to that is: and would they be willing to die for a lie?

Then there is the empty tomb: in itself it is a negative piece of evidence, but one that could easily have been disproved by the many enemies of the early Christians. Instead they had to resort to rumours that the believers stole the corpse (Matthew 28:15).

The more positive evidence comes from the apparitions or encounters with the Risen Jesus. But here there is something that goes against our expectations. Our 'objective' way of thinking would prefer an apparition to Pilate or to the crowds that called for his crucifixion. That would clinch matters! Instead what the gospels tell us is more a matter of faith than of public miracle. The Scriptures are blunt about this. In the words of St Peter, Jesus showed himself '*not* to all the people but to us who were chosen by God as witnesses, who ate and drank with him after he rose from the dead' (Acts 10:41).

That last phrase is a way of saying that it was not just a ghostly vision but a real bodily presence. But with some important differences. The Risen Jesus is not like Lazarus, revived from the dead and due to die again. Jesus did not return from the dead; he went through and beyond death. Or, as John's Gospel stresses, he returned to the Father and was not seen again in the same human way (16:10). With the Risen Jesus we are faced with an altogether new reality – at once an ordinary and physical presence with his old wounds, and yet different, changed, extraordinary – capable of passing through locked doors, and not immediately recognisable, even to his friends. Our expectations are being overturned: this is not Jesus as he walked in Galilee with them; instead it is Jesus in the fullness of divinity with the Father, and showing himself in what St Paul calls his 'glorious body' (Philippians 3:21). Interestingly, the Risen Jesus more than once uses a new greeting that he never used before his death: 'Peace be with you' (John 20:19). It sums up a whole new situation of victory and trust, something he shares with us as a gift.

Of course the Resurrection accounts in the gospels have been accused of confusion and discrepancies: for instance, do the apparitions take place in Jerusalem or Galilee? Or does the Ascension take place at Easter or forty days later? But there is no confusion about the earliest statement of Resurrection in the New Testament. Even before the gospels were given their final form, St Paul gave a very compressed summary of the appearances of the Risen Jesus, including a moment not mentioned in the gospels: 'He appeared to more than five hundred brethren at one time, most of whom are still alive' (1 Corinthians 15:6).

It is possible to study all these claims in the spirit of a detective or of a neutral historian and arrive at different conclusions: that the story makes sense, or else that it is impossible to believe. The philosopher Hume said that even if Queen Elizabeth I was reported to have come back from the dead to reign for three more months, and even if she had been seen by all her subjects, he would not believe it, simply because such a thing is impossible. If we approach the Resurrection in that spirit, rejection of it is a foregone conclusion. Even with a less prejudiced approach, a merely external inquiry is doomed to failure if the object is to arrive at faith in the Risen Jesus. We are talking about God acting in a unique way in Christ and to realise that involves more than weighing the evidence like a detective.

Why? Because, just like the first privileged witnesses, we need eyes of faith to see the amazing truth behind these signs, and because we are talking about an experience that changes everything. In the words of St Paul, 'the power of the Resurrection' means that we can 'walk in newness of life'. So the Resurrection is more than an external fact about Jesus: it is a promise to us too. Just as he died 'for us', he rose for us. Our own deepest desires are realised. Death is not the end. Love has won. Not just a consoling thought but the greatest surprise of God, the beginning of a new creation.

Let us return to the gospels, and find two points to conclude this answer. It is fascinating that in each Resurrection appearance, Jesus shows himself to his friends when they are in desolation of some kind – locked in an upper room because of fear, weeping at the tomb, walking away in despair, after a futile night of catching no fish, and so on. He is educating them, so to speak, not only about his victory over death but about his presence with them in everything, and especially in moments of darkness or doubt.

Then there is the famous story of 'doubting' Thomas. Leaving aside other issues, he refused to believe the witness of the others who saw the Lord. While he was absent from the community, he missed something. We can only believe in the Resurrection on the word of witnesses and we can best experience the Lord within the community of believers. Which Thomas did the second time. Looked at from the outside the Resurrection seems incredible. From within we find eyes to see and believe.

25   *Can we be sure of a life after death?*

Through faith in Christ and his Resurrection, yes. Through other avenues, no. By other avenues I mean anything from deceptive experiments in spiritualism to so-called 'after-death' experiences. Even the long tradition of philosophy about the 'immortality of the soul' is only impressive speculation compared with the promise of sharing Christ's own victory over death. We can tackle this question under a few headings, drawing on the Scriptures, which are our only real guide.

1. **Christian hope includes another life with Christ.**
   Nobody has been more blunt about this than St Paul, writing to the Church of Corinth, where some people doubted any 'resurrection from the dead'. If 'our hope in Christ has been for this life only', *then*, Paul draws four startling conclusions: a) it is like saying that Christ did not rise from the dead; b) there is no basis left for faith; c) if Christ is only a model for this life, believers are simply fools; d) so they should just live for present pleasures: 'eat and drink for tomorrow we die'. Against all these doubts is Paul's powerful proclamation of the Christian vision: 'In Christ all will be brought to life' (Corinthians 15:12-33).

2. **This rising from the dead involves the whole person transformed – like another birth.**
   For St Paul life beyond the grave is not some partial survival: 'We are going to be changed' and become 'a spiritual body' (1 Corinthians 15:44, 52). On this basis of a 'resurrection of the body' as the Creed says, the Church has always taught that we will 'enter into the joy of the Lord' (Matthew 25:23)

and find ourselves in the company of those we have loved in this life.

A traditional image for death is, paradoxically, birth. A child in the womb is utterly comfortable and knows nothing of the world outside this space. Then comes the terrifying moment of emergence into another world. It is a kind of death. But the fear and panic changes to contentment when the newborn discovers the presence of the mother. Death must be a bit like that, going into a different dimension and 'then we shall be seeing face to face' (1 Corinthians 13:12).

3. **In this life we can know little about that other reality.**
St Paul wrote that 'what no eye has seen and no ear has heard, what the human mind cannot imagine, all that God has prepared for those who love him' (1 Corinthians 2:9). Inevitably we want to imagine it, and we often fall into fantasy. Why? Because in this life *everything* is time and space, and life with God is beyond time and space. At the very end of the New Testament comes a marvellous passage about 'a new heaven and a new earth' which speaks of God wiping away all tears: 'There will be no more death...the world of the past has gone. Then the One sitting on the throne spoke, "Look, I am making the whole of creation new"' (Revelation 21:1-5).

4. **Eternity is another horizon, not just endless time.**
Going on and on for ever can only seem boring to us here: instead, eternity is some kind of permanent 'now' of newness which we cannot really imagine. There is a parable about eternity that I like: it tells of a medieval monk who found it hard to believe in eternal happiness because it seemed so monotonous. Once he wandered into a forest and heard the song of a nightingale. It was so beautiful that he stopped a long time just to listen and absorb it. When he got back to his monastery everything was completely altered and nobody

recognised him. In his confusion he gave them the name of his abbot, only to be told that this famous abbot had died a thousand years earlier! The point of this simple tale is that eternity is like moments when the heart is full of wonder, when, as we say, 'time stops'.

Perhaps stories help more than theories in this whole area. So I will risk recalling an experience of my own, to gather up the strands of this answer. Recently in Rome I had an X-ray to investigate a stomach problem. At one point the doctor in charge said to his assistant (perhaps thinking that I could not understand much Italian): 'There's something in that area – put in a bigger plate for an enlargement'. You can read everything into a little sentence like that! As I lay there, wondering if I had just heard my death sentence, I noticed a crucifix on the wall, and all I could think of was this: *If* I have something fatal, I believe I go this journey with Christ – through death into another way of being with him. As it happens there was nothing wrong with me but the small moment of panic forced on me the realisation that Christ went this way before me, and that one day I will cross this strange threshold of death *with him*, and find myself, I trust, with him in a totally new way. 'Because I live, you also will live', promised Jesus (John 14:19).

A postscript: Marxists used to accuse religion of being the 'opium of the people' and therefore diminishing the desire to change this world. The Second Vatican Council has a surprisingly strong comment that believers who shirk their 'temporal' responsibilities are endangering their 'eternal salvation' (*Gaudium et spes*, 43). In my own experience I think that mortality – the fact that we know our time is limited – makes each day precious and gives us a greater urgency to transform this world for others. To end with a paradox from Chesterton: 'false optimism' tries to make us feel at home here, whereas 'Christian optimism is based on the fact that we do not fit into the world'.

making. Before Galileo's time science thought of itself as looking for purpose in the universe. Then its approach shifted to verifying external data, and to being more interested in cause and effect than in some ultimate purpose. The very success of this 'empirical' method created the impression that there was no other road to truth. Taking an accurate look at reality was everything.

Thus science developed enormously but in a limited field: describing and even explaining particular aspects of the universe. However, that approach – Laplace was right – felt no need to ask bigger questions. As Hamlet says to his less imaginative friend, 'there are more things in heaven and earth, Horatio, than are dreamt of in your philosophy'. We come back to the central point about not confusing methods, and of remaining open to horizons not dreamt of in empirical science.

The road to scientific truth, if it stays on the level of observation, will not bring us to religious truth. They are different wavelengths of our humanity. Indeed, scientists have found that there are two hemispheres in our brain that work along different lines: the left brain specialises in clear and logical analysis but the right side is more intuitive and musical. Perhaps the very success of empirical science has caused us to equate truth with the 'left' approach only and to distrust that 'right' wavelength of our thinking.

In the last few decades huge changes have taken place within science and its relations with religion. The old method of Galileo and Newton is no longer central, at least for the frontiers of physics or astronomy. A more recent scientific method deals with what is beyond mere observation. What is called 'positivism' has gone into decline, meaning the approach that reduced all reality to surface visibility. I don't understand all the implications of 'relativity' or 'quantum mechanics' but I learn from scientists that the old separation between empirical and philosophical questions is out of date (Fr Gornall would be excited!). Science itself has become much more open to mystery.

Science, old and new, assumes that the world is somehow intelligible. Or, as Einstein himself remarked, 'the eternal mystery of the world is its comprehensibility'. But science today is much more aware of the limited nature of its hypotheses and, faced with the complexity of the cosmos, of how little is really certain. In such a situation (I borrow here from the physicist Polkinghorne) 'the ability of understanding to outrun explanation' is true both of advanced science and of religious faith.

Of course problems still arise today, mainly in relation to the application of technology (genetic engineering or ecology, for instance). In fact, because of these ethical problems a new mutual respect is developing between the Church and the world of science. The tone of this new dialogue is captured in the words of Pope John Paul II:

> Religion is not founded on science nor is science an extension of religion. Each should possess its own principles.... Science can purify religion from error and superstition; religion can purify science from idolatry and false absolutes. Each can draw the other into a wider world, a world in which both can flourish. (from a letter to Fr George Coyne)

So, that initial question seems out of date when we see the new horizons emerging today.